By Sidney and Carolyn Moss

Revised Edition

The New Composition by Logic

Southern Illinois University Press

Carbondale and Edwardsville

Feffer & Simons, Inc.

London and Amsterdam

Library of Congress Cataloging in Publication Data

Moss, Sidney Phil, 1917–
   The new Composition by logic.

   Edition for 1966 published under title: Composition by logic.
   Includes index.
   1. English language—Rhetoric. I. Moss, Carolyn, joint author. II. Title.
PE1408.M7   1978   808'.042   78-744
ISBN 0-8093-0857-6

pub. 8.29(8.95)
11/8/79

The student themes are printed here with permission of the writers, who also gave the authors *carte blanche* to adapt them to the purposes of this book.

The passage from *Catch-22* by Joseph Heller, copyright © 1955, 1961 by Joseph Heller, is reprinted here by permission of Jonathan Cape and Simon and Schuster, a Division of Gulf and Western Corporation.

The passage from *New Light on Romeo and Juliet* by George Lyman Kittredge, © 1942, is reprinted here by permission of The Club of Odd Volumes.

The passage from *The Personal World: An Introduction to the Study of Personality* by Harold McCurdy, © 1961 by Harcourt Brace Jovanovich, Inc., is reprinted here with their permission.

The passage from *Serving Through Science* by Henry Norris Russell, © 1946 by United States Rubber Co., is reprinted here by permission of Uniroyal, Inc.

The passages from *Life on the Mississippi*, *The Mysterious Stranger*, and *Roughing It* by Mark Twain are reprinted here by permission of Harper and Row.

To our former students, without whom this book
would not have been possible, or necessary

Contents

Preface

Face to face with an alien and overwhelming power, reflection can . . . ratio-nalize that power by conceiving its laws; and with this recognition of the ra-tionality of . . . things comes a sense of their beauty and order.
—George Santayana

If I have renounced the search for truth, if I have come into the port of some pretending dogmatism, . . . I am a bankrupt to whom brilliant opportunities are offered in vain.—Ralph Waldo Emerson

Whatever may be our views of students' educability, most of us will acknowl-edge that our freshmen do not really want to fail their composition courses, whether in grade or achievement, and that they seem ready and willing enough to apply the methodology we teach them. And whatever may be our views of our power to educate freshmen, most of us will agree that we do not really want our students to fail, and that we, in turn, stand ready and willing to help them master the principles of composition.

Why, then, given such quite positive conditions, do we tend to get such negative results, and why do we get them so repetitively, including disappoint-ment and even embitterment on both sides? The answer that leaps up at us is that the blame lies not so much with students and teachers as with the method-ology we have adopted, a methodology that with very little variation has been passed down to us from the turn of the last century.

What is offered here in its place is a fresh methodology whose least virtue is the demonstration that composition is an intriguing intellectual discipline that ranks among the most important courses in the curriculum.

It should be added that *The New Composition by Logic* derives from a book written by one of the authors and that, under the title *Composition by Logic*, was widely used in composition classes here and abroad.

Sidney and Carolyn Moss
Carbondale, Illinois
July 1977

Introduction

Composition is an intellectual discipline. What is meant by "intellectual discipline" is "game playing" of a high order. (The term "game" derives from the mathematical Theory of Games and refers to sequences of behavior which are governed by rules.) Anyone who has played games like basketball or chess knows that for a game to be a game it must impose certain conditions upon the players. First, it must have rules which, when violated, cause the player to "foul out." Secondly, a game must represent a test of an individual's physical or intellectual skill by offering a problem to be solved and an objective to be reached. In basketball, for instance, the main problem to be solved is how to put the ball through your opponents' basket as many times as possible within forty minutes at the same time that you are preventing your opponents from putting the ball through your basket. In chess, the problem is to checkmate your adversary's king at the same time that you are preventing your adversary from checkmating your king. The objective of both these games is to demonstrate superior ability.

Third, a game represents an abstract activity having to all appearances little or nothing to do with what we ordinarily call reality or real life. What, for instance, has a basketball or a chess game to do with reality? Nothing, if by "reality" we mean such practical activities as rearing a family and earning money. The true answer, however, is that games create their own reality and thus have their own good reasons for existing. The reality they create is very great if the game is played well; conversely, the reality they produce is very weak if the game is played poorly. Spectators, for instance, become astonishingly excited at watching a well-played basketball or chess game, but bored or even offended at watching a game poorly played.

As we have suggested, then, the act of composition is a game that can be of a high order indeed. When played well, writing ranks with mathematics (when mathematics is played well), with physics (when physics is played well), with biology (when biology is played well). In other words, the game of composition can be a significant form of intellectual activity or it can be trivial. What makes the difference is the skill one brings to the game and the zeal with which one plays.

Composition, to repeat, is a game in that it imposes certain conditions upon the players; it represents a test of intellectual skill by offering a problem to be solved and an objective to be achieved; and, though abstract, creates its own reality which, if vivid enough, provokes a significant response from the reader, but which, if weak, produces only boredom in him.

The rules imposed upon players of the composition game are well known and need little discussion here. These rules have to do with "mechanics"—grammar, spelling, punctuation, and the like. Less well known is the kind of problem that writing poses for the player and the objective he is to achieve. The problem is largely a psychological one: to find an effective way of externalizing the cluster of ideas, feelings, and information the writer has about a given subject. To be more precise, when a topic arises for discussion, we have certain reactions which are vague and miscellaneous. Our purpose in writing is to express those reactions in a way that mirrors them faithfully but that does not reflect their original vagueness and miscellaneousness. In short, the test of skill lies in objectifying on paper what exists subjectively within ourselves so that others may share our experiences, our sense of reality. This is not easy to do well, as every "beginner" knows, for a number of reasons. First, the act of writing represents a translation from the private and anarchic "language" and "logic" of the inner self (the "language" of images, for example, and the "logic" of free association) into the public and "legislated" language and logic of the outer or conscious self. Moreover, the cluster of ideas, feelings, and information we have about a given subject exists "all at once" in a state of "here and now"; yet in writing we must express such reactions as if they existed singly and occurred to us one after another in successive order. Thus, one might well wonder how anyone manages to mirror his "real" feelings and thoughts about a subject at all.

This leads to the third point, that writing is an abstraction—not an expression of our real thoughts and feelings but an intimation of them, a condensation of them, in which we try to catch their *quality*, not their *quantity*. Nevertheless, as we have suggested, the reality created by such "translations" has been and will continue to be significant. People can be far more stirred by the plays of Sophocles and Shakespeare, by the Bible, by *Walden*, by even such short pieces as the Gettysburg Address, than they can by real-life occurrences. The very condensation which such works represent, and their ordering of random ideas, feelings, and information, produce at once a dramatic intensity and a view of experience that "real" thoughts and feelings seldom do. But we need not stretch ourselves so far to appreciate the reality that writing creates. Anyone who has read fairy tales as a child knows what a vivid sense of reality can be induced in him by the written word. Anyone who has been torn away from an engrossing book by the sound of his mother's voice calling him to the table knows that the spell of reality which a composition can cast is infinitely greater than that which usually confronts him at the dinner table.

The question arises as to whether everyone's thoughts and feelings are worth expressing—worth the effort of dredging up from below-conscious levels and formulating on the conscious level. The answer to that question depends in great measure upon what might be called an X factor: a person's sensitivity to experience, his power of syntax and diction to express his sensitivity, his awareness of the world in which he lives, an inquisitiveness as to what brought him to this point in time and space, and—connected with all this—his interest in emotional and intellectual problems. No one, as a psychology teacher told a student who came to him for counsel, can give us a new nervous system or miraculously enrich our background, but we can at least develop the nervous system we do have and enrich the background we do possess so that what we have to say can be of greater interest to others.

Another question that arises is why do we, those of us who have no intention of becoming professional writers, try to solve the composition problem at all? After all, it is a game that not everyone enjoys playing. There are many answers to this question, not all of equal value for everyone, but that, taken together, are of the utmost value. Practically speaking, competence in every profession demands clear explanations: how we performed an experiment and what results we achieved; why one view of an historical character or a cultural situation is sounder than another. Humanistically speaking, we are all social beings and as such have a responsibility to ourselves and others to express our states of mind with some fidelity to their contents. Psychologically speaking, the act of writing enables us to know ourselves. To paraphrase William James, writing allows the *I* to observe the *Me* in that the *I* searches out the *Me* that exists in an elusive, shadowy, and rather formless state and fixes it in a substantial and inspectable form on paper. Furthermore, writing accustoms us to the practice of examining our reactions to a given topic to see whether they are indeed sound—based, that is, upon solid emotional and intellectual ground—or whether they are merely the result of conditioning. Such a practice can elevate us from a subcerebral, animal-like level, on which we can be easily manipulated, to the full status of human beings who have the gift of reason and a hand in our destinies. Some men, like Plato, Spinoza, and Emerson, try to search out "the absolute order of things as they stand in the mind of God" instead of permitting themselves to be the victims of local prejudice or merely prevailing ideas—one reason, certainly, why these men still command immense respect.

Since the principal object of writing is to share our emotional and intellectual responses to experience with our readers, we need to render their quality and to order their presentation. In doing this, we can proceed to the solution on the conscious level, by reason; or, on the less than conscious level, by chance. In actual practice, of course, reason *and* chance play significant roles, and we in no way wish to suppress the happy spontaneities that chance often offers to reason. Our only objection is to the anarchy that chance frequently introduces. Thus, if in the discussion that follows, we attempt to lift writing from the less than conscious level to the conscious level, to emphasize the effects to be achieved by reason rather than those achieved by chance, no one should assume that we are trying to repress inspiration, or what Alexander Pope called "the grace beyond the reach of art." The truth is that unless we draw upon the vast resources of the subconscious, we could not write at all. All we urge anyone to do, then, is to master those resources to a greater degree, not to be victimized by them. Thus, what we are really concerned about is to demonstrate the advantages to be gained from conscious effort, from imposing order upon randomness—from, in short, controlling the ideas, feelings, and information that rise, bidden and unbidden, from below the conscious levels. To accomplish this, we shall now begin to explain the game of composition, a game that by virtue of being a *game*, requires certain sequences of behavior governed by rules.

1 The Organization of Themes

Why Topics

This book takes the stand that every theme and essay is an exercise in persuasion. Thus, whether the subject is "The probable landscape of Mars," or "How Louis Pasteur discovered the principle of vaccination," or "Attendance of college classes ought to be voluntary," the writer is to hold himself responsible for presenting his case in such a way as to persuade his readers that the Martian landscape is most likely as he has described it; that Louis Pasteur no doubt discovered the principle of vaccination in the way the writer has explained it; that the attendance problem at college is worth reconsidering in the light of the writer's discussion. In each of these instances, the writer seeks to persuade his readers by writing in such a way that they share his sense of reality about a scene (the Martian landscape), a discovery (the vaccination principle), or a conviction (voluntary attendance of college classes). This sharing of one's sense of reality with readers is the object of all writing. The degree to which this is accomplished is the difference between high art and low art.

In addition, this book takes the stand that all essay and theme topics are of two basic kinds, herein called *why* topics and *what* topics. A *why* topic calls for an **opinion plus information** about that topic. In discussing a *why* topic, therefore, one draws in large measure upon the *private domain*—upon one's personal attitudes and upon information that he has personalized. For example, the topic, "Why I advocate (oppose) censoring movies" or "Why I oppose (advocate) socializing the American oil industry" will elicit a great variety of personal responses.

What topics, on the other hand, call, not for opinion, but for **information only**, and one draws in great measure upon the *public domain*—upon information that, for the most part, is found in print—in books, magazines, newspapers, and pamphlets. In discussing a *what* topic, the information presented is generally uniform. For example, the topic "What are some current treatments of cancer?" or "What are the Catholic sacraments?" will elicit fairly uniform information.

An easy test of whether we are presented with a *why* topic or a *what* topic is this: Can a position differing from ours be *reasonably* taken toward the topic? If so, we have a *why* topic. If no differing position can be *reasonably* taken, we have a *what* topic. To be sure, differing positions from ours can always be taken, even when what we assert seems undeniable fact; thus, the operative word is *reasonably*. The point is that *why* topics are controversial and *what* topics are not controversial.

Since all theme and essay topics are of the *why* and *what* class, it follows that all other forms are only permutations or combinations of these two basic forms. Questions of *where*, *when*, and *who* are of little concern, since they usually call for brief comment and these comments are typically incorporated into the body of themes and essays.

The presence of the words *why* or *what* in the statement of the topic can be deceptive. For example, "*What* do you think about legalizing marijuana?" is not a *what* topic at all, since it calls for opinion and personalized information, and a differing opinion from ours is possible. Likewise, "*Why* was General Douglas MacArthur relieved of his command during the Korean War?" is not a *why* topic, since it calls for information in the public domain (any departure from the facts would be an error). Therefore, instead of relying upon such linguistic clues as *why* and *what*, we need to concentrate upon what the topic is essentially asking us to do.

Exercises A: **Distinguishing WHY** **Topics from WHAT** **Topics**	Here are examples of *why* and *what* topics, all of which begin with the word *what*. Separate the *why* from the *what* topics and give your reasons for doing so.

   1. What are some themes in Poe's fiction?
   2. What are T. S. Eliot's views of Poe in his essay "From Poe to Valéry"?*
   3. What are your reasons for agreeing or disagreeing with T. S. Eliot's views of Poe in his essay, "From Poe to Valéry"?
   4. What is your attitude toward censoring X-rated movies?
   5. What is the history of *Playboy*?
   6. What is your conception of a great teacher?
   7. What were the successive discoveries of America?
   8. What is your opinion concerning no-fault insurance?
   9. What did Florence Nightingale do during the Crimean War?

A topic is sometimes introduced, not by the words *why* or *what*, but by such words as *explain*, *discuss*, *is*, or *are*; or, even more simply, by merely a statement of the topic itself. See *Exercises B* below.

Exercises B: **Various Ways of** **Expressing WHY and** **WHAT Topics**	Examine the topics below and sort out the *what* and *why* topics.

1. Discuss your views of the Feminist Movement.
2. Discuss your opinion of the Mexican War of 1846.
3. Should doctors have the right to strike?
4. Should the United States have become involved in the Vietnamese War? (*Or*: On the involvement of the United States in the Vietnamese War)
5. Are standards for the driver's license sufficiently high in my state? (*Or*: Should the standards for the driver's license be raised in my state?)
6. Should policemen have the right to strike? (*Or*: On the right of policemen to strike)
7. Should final examinations be eliminated at my college? (*Or*: On eliminating final examinations at my college)

---

*The views, opinions, and arguments *of others* that we cite in our themes are to be considered as facts, so long as we do not distort them. It is a fact that T. S. Eliot expressed certain views about Poe in the essay cited. Likewise, it is a fact that more voters had the opinion in 1972 that Richard Nixon would be a better president than George McGovern.

8. Discuss the major civil-rights activities of Martin Luther King, Jr.
9. The origin of the Teamsters' Union.

Stage One in Writing WHY Themes: The Thesis

The first thing to do in writing a *why* theme is to state your opinion of the subject in the form of a *thesis*. (A *thesis* for a *why* topic is defined as an unexplained opinion.) Below appear some examples of *why* topics and of theses drawn from them.

Examples A: WHY Topics and Theses	**Topics**	**Theses**
	Discuss your views of fraternities and sororities	Social fraternities and sororities should be outlawed from college campuses.
	The right of doctors to strike.	Doctors should not be allowed to strike.
	Should private corporations be subsidized by our government?	No private corporation should be subsidized by our government.
	Should high schools have a five-year program?	All high schools should inaugurate a five-year program.

Exercises C

1. How would you assert the negation of each of the theses in *Examples A* above?
2. With which of the theses do you intuitively agree? Disagree?
3. Cite one reason for agreeing or disagreeing with each of the theses.

In writing *why* theses one has to avoid four major kinds of intellectual errors. These kinds of errors, together with examples and explanations, are specified in *Examples B* below.

Examples B:
Errors in WHY Theses

1. Undemonstrable Theses

a. Given time, Benjamin Franklin would have anticipated Albert Einstein in formulating the Theory of Relativity.

Such a thesis is not proper for themes since it cannot be supported by evidence, but only by guesswork concerning Franklin's intellectual, psychological, and cultural possibilities.

b. Salvation can only be attained by good works.

Such a thesis is also not proper for themes, since it cannot be supported except by special interpretation of selected Biblical texts. There is no objection, of course, to matters of faith, but themes requiring persuasive evidence and reasoning are not the occasions for professing such matters.

2. Nonspecific WHY Theses

a. Colleges should be made harder to enter.
b. Some wars are bad.

Such theses should be stated precisely. Which college should be made harder to enter—yours, colleges like Harvard and Yale, or all colleges? Similarly, which wars are bad—revolutions like the American, French, Russian, and Cuban revolutions, or world wars?

3. WHAT Theses Mistaken for WHY Theses

   a. There are many diseases that still kill animals and people.

   b. *X* is the governor of my state

   c. I like to watch football.

As was said on page 3, an easy test of whether we have a *why* thesis or a *what* thesis is to determine if a position differing from ours can be reasonably taken toward the topic. If a differing position can be reasonably taken, we have a *why* thesis. If a differing position cannot be reasonably taken, we have a *what* thesis. Can anyone, for instance, reasonably argue with any of the above theses?

4. Multiple Theses

   a. The United States government should enforce the civil-rights laws with greater rigor and should strive for peace in the world.

   b. The South ought not to have seceded from the Union, nor raised cotton on such a wide scale, nor waged civil war.

While these theses promise to be controversial, each of them commits the writer to composing more than one theme, for which—certainly in a single class session—he may not have time.

Exercises D: Undemonstrable, Non-specific, WHAT for WHY, Multiple, and Proper WHY Theses

In which category (the categories are specified in the margin) would you put each of the theses given below? (In doing this exercise, ignore the possibility that multiple theses can be integrated in an extended essay or book.)

1. Divorce laws should be less stringent. *Nonspecific*
2. Everyone on public welfare is a chiseler. *Undemonstrable. Everyone is too many to talk to*
3. Without love there can be no life.
4. I like skin diving. *what for why*
5. The United States Army should do away with its caste system of officers and noncommissioned officers, and American colleges should do away with professorial ranks. *Multiple theses*
6. I want to be a physics teacher. *what for why*
7. All students in my college should be required to study at least three years of mathematics. *proper*
8. Some people are thoughtful. *non specific*
9. Employment in trades and professions should be proportional to the ethnic and sexual composition of the population. *proper*
10. I like my roommate. *what, not why*
11. Shakespeare had a guilt complex. *Undemonstrable*
12. Fire can cause very severe burns. *what for why*
13. There should be no censorship of books. *proper*

Trivialization of WHY Theses

Authenticity

However significant theses may sound, they can be trivialized. To trivialize is to reduce that which is intellectually interesting to that which is intellectually uninteresting. A theme is judged to be excellent, mediocre, or inferior, not merely on the grounds that it is "correctly" or "incorrectly" written, but on the grounds of its triviality or significance. Trivialization often occurs when the thesis is *inauthentic for the writer*—when, in short, the subject does not engage his intellectual interests. To explain: if you write a thesis such as "All atomic weapons should be destroyed within the next decade," you are promising, in effect, to provide persuasive evidence and reasoning to support that thesis. If you fulfill this promise in your theme, you will have demonstrated that your thesis is *authentic for you*. If, however, you do not or cannot provide persuasive evidence and reasoning to support your thesis, you will have demonstrated that the thesis was *inauthentic* for you. Given these results, you obviously should not write theses that are inauthentic for you.

Exercises E

1. What is meant by *evidence*? By *reasoning*? (An intuitive answer is all that you need give at this point. However, a full discussion of evidence and the process of reasoning appears in the second section of this book.)
2. What is meant by an *authentic* thesis?
3. Write three authentic *Why* theses of your own creation that avoid the four kinds of intellectual errors shown in *Examples B*. Be sure that your theses are perfect in regard to spelling and punctuation. Title your paper: Three Authentic *Why* Theses.

Stage Two in Writing WHY Themes: From Thesis to Thesis Sentence

Earlier, on page 3, we made some intuitive remarks about *why* topics. But there is a more interesting and useful way of looking at *why* topics. That way is to see a *why* topic as a **set** containing subsets, which, in turn, contain one or more elements. Don't let these terms trouble you; they are quite simple. A *set* is simply another word for class, or collection, or category; *subsets* are simply subdivisions of a set; *elements* are simply members of a subset. For example, your English class constitutes a set. How many members or elements does that set have? Your teacher as a teacher is a member of a set. What set is that? Some sets contain a limited number of members—the set of "all-A" students who have graduated from your college, for instance. (If there were no members in this set—no "all-A" students, in other words—we would call this a null or empty set, which is to say, the set exists but has no members.) Some sets have a great number of elements—the set of your college, for instance, especially if it is part of a big university. Other sets contain an extraordinarily large number of elements, such as the sets of married and divorced people.

sets & subset

As we said, sets are also subsets of other sets. In fact, all subsets except "the set of the whole" are subsets. For instance, a married couple in your English class belongs to the set of married people as well as to the subsets of your college's enrollees and of your class. To what other subsets might this married couple belong?

All intellectual disciplines require such classification. In fact, whether we are aware of the process or not, we are all classifiers. For example, a child at first tends to divide the set of *men* into two subsets: (1) father and (2) all other men. As the child becomes more intelligent, more aware of the world about him (as evidenced by his developing ability to classify), he subdivides the set of *men* in subtler ways—by jobs, for instance. Thus, he has sets for newspapermen, grocerymen, mailmen, television repairmen, foundrymen, dairymen, garbage men, and so forth. As he becomes still more aware of his world (to take only one of these subsets), he further subdivides newspapermen into cub reporters, reporters, editors, foreign correspondents, and so on through the ranks.

The Two Subsets of a WHY Topic

A *why* topic contains two subsets: (1) a *positive* subset and its elements and (2) a *negative* subset and its elements. The positive subset and its elements affirm a given position (e.g., "A doctor should have the right to terminate human life under certain medical and moral conditions"). The negative subset and its elements deny a given position (e.g., "A doctor should not have the right to terminate human life whatever medical and moral conditions prevail"). To clarify this discussion, consider the positive and negative subsets analyzed below.

Positive Subset

Set (specified as **why** topic)	Subset (specified as **thesis**)	Representative Subsets of the Subset
The right of a doctor to terminate human life	A doctor should have the right to terminate human life . . .	. . . under certain medical and moral conditions. (*medical conditions* might include such elements as (1) doctor is the best authority on when to terminate life; (2) hospital facilities used in maintaining vital signs in an incurable person might be needed to help others recover; etc. *moral conditions* might include such elements as (1) letting a person suffer futilely; (2) denying a person his right to die; (3) pointlessly draining the family of money; etc.)

Negative Subset

Set (specified as **why** topic)	Subset (specified as **thesis**)	Representative Subsets of the Subset
The right of a doctor to terminate human life	A doctor should not have the right to terminate human life . . .	. . . whatever medical and moral conditions prevail. (*medical conditions* might include such elements as (1) the doctor's medical task is to maintain life, not take it; (2) the patient's suffering is not wasted in that it adds to medical knowledge; (3) a cure may be found; etc. *moral conditions* might include such elements as (1) taking life sets a dangerous precedent for society; (2) the privilege to deal out death can be easily abused when wealth and power are involved; etc.)

Which subset to adopt—the positive or negative—and which elements to select to represent that subset is an intellectual decision that we have to make. Clearly, if we have formed no opinion on the subject, as would be evident from our having little familiarity with the elements of the topic, we ought not to write on the topic at all, at least not before familiarizing ourselves with it. Otherwise, our thesis would be inauthentic and, in consequence, we would trivialize the subject.

The above analysis can be simplified considerably if we adopt a few symbols, namely, S and $l \ldots n$. S will stand for *subset* (positive or negative) and $l \ldots n$ (n designates an unspecified *n*umber) will stand for either the subsets of the subset *or* the elements, both of which constitute **reasons** for affirming S. Thus, the sentence "A doctor should have the right to terminate human life under certain medical and moral conditions" can be expressed symbolically as "S because of 1 and 2." Any sentence that verbalizes the formula "S because of $l \ldots n$" and that appears as the first sentence in a theme shall be called a *thesis sentence*. (We use expressions like *because, since, for, for these reasons*, and *under these conditions* to establish the relationship between S and $l \ldots n$ inasmuch as $l \ldots n$ represent *reasons* of the subset. *Because* is used frequently in the examples only to emphasize the relationship between S and $l \ldots n$, but equivalent expressions may be substituted at will.) Thesis sentences that can be described by the formula "S because of $l \ldots n$" appear in *Examples C*.

Examples C: **Thesis Sentences**	1. Social fraternities and sororities should be outlawed from college campuses because they are very expensive, they make too many demands on one's time, and they discriminate against certain students. 2. Doctors should not be allowed to strike because striking violates their Hippocratic oath, creates a hazard to public health, and encourages public officials to strike. 3. No private corporation should be subsidized by our government because such subsidies come from consumers' taxes, give undue power to the government, and interfere with our free-enterprise system. 4. All high schools should inaugurate a five-year program because such a program would better prepare the student for the vigorous college curriculum, allow him to become more mature so that he can adapt himself more readily to college, and give him more time to decide on his career.
Exercises F	1. What is meant by the terms *set* and *subset*? 2. Explain why a *why* topic is considered a set containing two subsets. 3. What do the symbols *l . . . n* designate? 4. On theme paper copy the four thesis sentences in *Examples C* above. Underline each *S* twice and each reason once. (Ignore the words *because* and *and*, which are only devices used for linking.) 5. Contrast the *thesis sentences* in *Examples C* above with the theses in *Examples A* (page 5). Which form is more likely to persuade you—the mere assertion (e.g., "Doctors should not be allowed to strike") or the partially explained assertion (e.g., "Doctors should not be allowed to strike because striking violates their Hippocratic oath, creates a hazard to public health, and encourages public officials to strike")?

Parallelism in the Thesis Sentence

The proper formulation of a thesis sentence depends upon two principles. The first is *parallelism*, which has both a grammatical and a logical function; the second is *relevance*, which has only a logical function.

Grammatical parallelism in the thesis sentence is established when each reason in the numerical series (*l . . . n*) begins with the same part of speech (stated or understood). Below is a grammatical analysis of two thesis sentences you have already dealt with.

Examples D: **Analysis of** **Grammatical** **Parallelism** **in the l . . . n Series**	**Thesis sentence** Social fraternities and sororities should be outlawed from college campuses because *they are very expensive*, *they make too many demands on one's time*, and *they discriminate against certain students*. 1. they are (pronoun plus verb) 2. they make (pronoun plus verb) 3. they discriminate (pronoun plus verb)

Thesis sentence

Doctors should not be allowed to strike because *striking violates their Hippo-cratic oath*, *creates a hazard to public health*, and *encourages public officials to strike*.

1. striking violates (noun plus verb)
2. (striking) creates (noun understood plus verb)
3. (striking) encourages (noun understood plus verb)

Exercise G

On theme paper copy the remaining two thesis sentences in *Examples C* (page 10) and subject them to the same grammatical analysis as has been done above.

Examples E:
Parallel and Unparallel
Thesis Sentences

Which of the examples below violate grammatical parallelism? Rewrite them so that the reasons in the *I . . . n* series are parallel.

1. Many students fail in college because they neglect to study and they party too much.
2. It is a privilege to eat in the college cafeteria because the food is delicious, they serve large portions, and the cost.
3. Girls attending college should live in dormitories because there are many opportunities to meet people and the regulations.
4. Long-range patrol planes should not be abandoned because they help to pinpoint hurricanes and are capable of carrying large warheads.
5. Pay television is good because it offers a finer selection of programs and constrains the regular TV networks to show better programs also.

Exercises H

1. Write two authentic thesis sentences of your own creation and subject them to grammatical analysis.
2. In the light of your analysis, are your reasons grammatically parallel? If not, rewrite them so that they are grammatically parallel.

Should you experience any difficulty in mastering grammatical parallelism, you are advised to state each reason in the numerical series with verbal fullness and then delete the redundant words. The example below with its revision shows how parallelism can be accomplished in this way:

No corporation should be subsidized by our government because such subsidies come from consumers' taxes, ~~because such subsidies~~ give undue power to the government, and ~~because such subsidies~~ interfere with our free-enterprise system.

Logical Parallelism in the Thesis Sentence

We said earlier that parallelism is not only a grammatical principle but a logical one also. This principle can be easily satisfied if you observe *two conditions*. First, specify a reason in the *I . . . n* series *only once*. "Disciplines the mind," "develops the intellect," and "cultivates the reason" obviously represent one reason that has been specified three times in this thesis sentence: "Three years of mathematics should be required of every undergraduate because the subject disciplines the mind, develops the intellect, and cultivates the reason." Similarly, "trivial" and "banal" represent the identical reason in this thesis sentence: "Students should not be required to register for course *x* because it is trivial and banal."

Secondly, specify your reasons either as subset *or* elements, *not both*, in the *l . . . n* series. For instance, "the entire range of human responses" is a subset that obviously includes the element "people often feel rejected" in this thesis sentence: "College students ought to study psychology because the subject gives them insight into the entire range of human responses and teaches them that people often feel rejected." The way to correct this non-parallelism in logic is to substitute a subset for the element ("people often feel rejected") or an element for the subset ("entire range of human responses"), as shown below.

Making the l . . . n series all subsets
College undergraduates ought to study psychology because the subject gives them insight into the entire range of normal and abnormal human responses.

Making the l . . . n series all elements
College undergraduates ought to study psychology because the subject gives them insight into the problem of rejection and confirmation.

Exercises I

In the thesis sentences below (a) explain which subsets or elements in the *l . . . n* series satisfy and which violate the *logical* function of parallelism and (b) revise each flawed instance so that it does satisfy the *logic* of parallelism.

1. A college education ought to be required of every adult because it would prepare him for a profession and teach him what he needs to know to enter that profession.
2. Clarence Darrow ought to be considered Christ-like because he materially helped the defenseless in court and spiritually enlightened the world about the virtue of compassion.
3. High school graduates ought to go to college for academic reasons, economic reasons, and to make friends.
4. American communists should be allowed to teach in college because their civil rights are protected by the Constitution and they have the right of free speech.

Relevance in the Thesis Sentence

The second principle that needs to be observed is *relevance*. *Relevance* is a logical principle that is easy to understand, since gross violations of it make for absurdity. Here is an example that is deliberately made absurd: "Candidate *X* will be a great president because yesterday I flew a kite and put my clothes in mothballs." Notice that this statement satisfies the conditions of the thesis sentence in all other respects: it is a sentence consisting of a controversial thesis, a *because* (though an equivalent expression would serve), a *1* and a

2, and it satisfies grammatical and logical parallelism. But *1* and *2*, though no doubt true, fail to provide grounds for the thesis since *1* and *2* are unrelated (irrelevant) to the thesis. To be more precise, *1* and *2* are not elements of *S*.

Exercises J

Explain in detail which of the thesis sentences below satisfy the principle of *relevance* and which violate that principle.

1. Mr. Smith would be an outstanding presidential candidate because he has a family, a good credit rating, and averages a low golf score.
2. Miss Jones is not a good teacher because she is an untidy housekeeper, a divorcée, and is not a church member.
3. Carl Sandburg was a great poet because he was poor, wrote a biography of Abraham Lincoln, and lived in Illinois.
4. By and large the American character has deteriorated since the time of Thomas Jefferson because Americans have lost much of their pride in property, their sense of integrity, and their love for their country.
5. Samuel Taylor Coleridge cannot be considered a great poet because he took opium and, though married, was in love with Wordsworth's sister.

Figurative Language in the Thesis Sentence

A last principle is that we need to avoid figurative language in the thesis sentence. *Figurative language* designates such figures of speech as personifications, metaphors, similes, and allusions (see pages 55–57). Though figurative language is desirable in appropriate contexts, it is not to be used in the thesis sentence because it proves confusing. The following example, made obviously absurd, indicates the reason for avoiding figurative language in the thesis sentence: "The subsidization of corporations by the United States is an attempt to make a donkey look like a gazelle, but it puts gloves on cats that are supposed to catch mice."

It may be taken as a rule that whatever failures occur in the thesis sentence (whether of an intellectual or a grammatical nature) will recur in magnification in the theme itself, for the theme is only an enlargement of the thesis sentence.

Definition of a Thesis Sentence

We have now reached the point at which the thesis sentence can be descriptively and functionally defined. (If any word or statement in this definition is obscure, you are urged to review this chapter carefully, since it is the foundation of the entire book.) Descriptively, the thesis sentence for a *why* topic is **a sentence consisting of a controversial thesis supported by a series of specified relevant reasons that satisfy the principles of grammatical and logical parallelism while avoiding figurative language.** Functionally, the thesis sentence for a *why* topic is simply **a rapid means of reconstructing and outlining the thought process by which we arrived at a given position.**

Exercise K

A person who can adduce reasonable grounds for a thesis is one who has obviously cultivated his mind. There are some persons, however, who have not had the opportunity to cultivate their minds in this way. To facilitate the development of this ability, your teacher may want to play a game in class that can be very productive. The game should begin in an elementary way at the outset. A student should suggest any idea that is controversial ("Abortion," for instance) and another student should respond, "Abortions should (should not) be legalized in the United States because of *l . . . n*." The precise reasons need not be specified at this stage of the game; the prime concern is to establish the controversiality of theses and to get the class to recognize that theses are to be supported by reasons. Once the class develops a facility with this phase of the game, the game can be made more sophisticated. First, one reason for the thesis may be offered by an individual, with additional reasons offered by the class collectively. The teacher or a student can, in the process, write the reasons on the blackboard and analyze them to determine if they are parallel (both logically and grammatically) and relevant. The game can be concluded when everyone has demonstrated that he is individually capable of adducing at least two reasons for two or three *why* topics that have been mentioned.

Stage Three: Organizing the Whole Theme

The symbols *l . . . n* designate not only the reasons for affirming or denying *S*, but also the *order* in which those reasons are to be arranged in the thesis sentence and discussed in the theme itself. One must choose, therefore, the order which is most logical in the circumstances. For *why* thesis sentences the choices are limited to three: (1) *random arrangement*, (2) *climactic arrangement*, and (3) *simple-to-complex arrangement*. *Random arrangement* may be used when *l . . . n* are of equal emotional value for the writer and when an understanding of one reason is not required for an understanding of another reason. For example, in the thesis sentence "The Peace Corps is of great medical help to the poor people abroad because it provides modern medical treatment for diseases and introduces better methods of sanitation to prevent disease," 1 and 2 could legitimately be reversed. Both reasons are of equal emotional value and an understanding of one is in no way dependent upon an understanding of the other.

Climactic arrangement, however, should be used when *l . . . n* have unequal emotional value for the writer. In such instances the reason having the least emotional value appears first, the reason having more emotional value appears next, and the reason having the most emotional value appears last. The arrangement of the reasons in the following thesis sentence shows that the writer feels that "time" has more emotional value than "expense," and that "discrimination" has more emotional value than either "expense" or "time": "Social fraternities and sororities should be outlawed from college campuses because they are very expensive, they make too many demands on one's time, and they discriminate against certain students."

Simple-to-complex arrangement should be used when a discussion of 1 makes it easier for you to explain and for your reader to understand your discussion of 2. Consider such a thesis sentence as this: "Pay television is good because it offers a finer selection of programs and constrains the regular TV networks to show better programs also." If one were to begin with 2, his theme would be unnecessarily complicated both for him and his reader.

Once the *order* of the reasons is determined in the thesis sentence, the *arrangement* of the reasons in the body of the theme becomes automatic. Thus, if the thesis sentence is the first paragraph in the theme, *1* will be the *implied* or *stated topic sentence* of the second paragraph; *2* of the third paragraph; *3* of the fourth; and so on. (A *topic sentence* is the controlling idea of a paragraph and is to the paragraph what the thesis sentence is to the entire theme. An *implied* topic sentence is one that must be inferred from the details of the paragraph, since it is not stated.)

Exercises L

1. Explain *random arrangement* and the nonrandom arrangements we have called *climactic arrangement* and *simple-to-complex arrangement*.
2. What is meant by *topic sentence*? When is a topic sentence said to be *implied*? When *stated*?
3. As you read the two themes below, spot each explicit (stated) topic sentence. If the topic sentence is implicit (implied), reconstruct the topic sentence from the paragraph itself.

Two Themes Exemplifying Thesis-Sentence Organization of WHY Topics*

WHY SOCIAL FRATERNITIES AND SORORITIES SHOULD BE OUTLAWED FROM COLLEGE CAMPUSES

Social fraternities and sororities should be outlawed from college campuses because they are very expensive, they make too many demands on one's time, and they discriminate against certain students.

Sheer expense often prohibits one from joining a social fraternity or sorority. After the initial expense of pledging, a student must spend still more money in order to retain his membership. Dues, usually levied monthly, must be paid on time lest a penalty fee be added to the original amount owed. Nor are these expenses all. The many functions sponsored by the fraternity or sorority are attended by members at their own expense. If one is a boy, he has the additional expense of a date. If a girl, her expenses involve, among other things, her clothes and her hair set. If all such expenses were lumped together, they would represent a very large sum of money that could be more usefully spent on books, records, prints, and the like.

Another problem involved in joining a social fraternity or sorority, one that is even more serious for the college student, is the great amount of time spent in what are seldom important or even amusing activities. For students who belong to social fraternities and sororities are required to support their clubs or all but perish in the effort. They are obliged to attend all meetings, for

*These student themes were developed from two of the thesis sentences already presented. The themes were written extemporaneously during a fifty-minute class session and were selected because they satisfy the conditions of thesis-sentence organization.

rather stiff fines are levied against those who miss meetings. Aside from these regular events, a social fraternity or sorority sponsors many other activities which its members are supposed to attend, not the least of which are the parties, closed and open, that are held with fair regularity during a given year. Members are also expected to spend time in building floats, in helping with projects designed to raise money, and in producing shows for the clubs. All loyal, upstanding members must participate, not in one, two, or three of such events, but in all of them. The cost in time often results in low grades because members spend less time on their studies than they should.

But the worst thing about social fraternities and sororities is that they admit only those students they want to. Sometimes a person may want to join a fraternity or a sorority, regardless of the expense and time involved. To be rejected by such a club can often leave a psychic scar. The applicant is made aware of the fact that his being a member of a minority group is enough to debar him, or that he is debarred merely because one or two members happen not to like him. These rejections can hurt deeply and are in themselves legitimate reasons for outlawing these discriminatory clubs from campuses that pride themselves upon observing the principles of democracy.

WHY HIGH SCHOOLS SHOULD INAUGURATE A FIVE-YEAR PROGRAM

All high schools should inaugurate a five-year program because such a program would better prepare the student for the vigorous college curriculum, allow him to become more mature so that he can adapt himself more readily to college, and give him more time to decide on his career.

Most students entering college are not fully prepared for the college subjects which they are required to study. If the high school program were extended from four to five years, the student would have more time to prepare himself for these more demanding subjects by taking a greater variety of courses and by learning to think more effectively. For example, I have already discovered during the few weeks I have been in college that I am very poorly prepared to study chemistry and mathematics and that I have a very weak background in history. Furthermore, I seem to learn more by rote than by thinking through a problem.

I have also discovered during the short time I have been in college that all too many freshmen are not mature enough to adapt to the college community. This is proved by the high rate of those who either drop out, fail out, or are put on academic probation during their freshman year. Some of these students fail because they do not have the intelligence to pass. But the larger number of those who fail, fail because they are not mature enough to realize that college is challenging and that, to be able to pass their courses, they need to study. These students are called "goof-offs" for good reason, and it is these very people who do damage, not only to themselves, but to other students and to the college itself. They are the ones who create confusion in the dormitories, who demoralize classes by their lack of preparation, and who bring a bad reputation to the college. If these students were required to study an additional year in high school, they would be older and, one hopes, more mature upon entering college, a fact that would enable them to adjust more easily to the college environment.

Furthermore, a large number of freshmen do not know what they want to do after they graduate from college, something that accounts for their foundering. They take any subject that they think might be easy and avoid those that are not absolutely required. Thus, when they do decide upon their major, they find that they have many subjects which they cannot count toward graduation or that have even proved useful. The sudden recognition of this fact causes them to become discouraged, in consequence of which many drop out of college altogether. If these students were required to study another year in high school, preferably college preparatory courses, they would have more time and opportunity to decide upon their vocation instead of wasting their time, their money, and, not least, themselves while they are in college.

In examining these specimen themes, notice that, whatever their defects, they are thoroughly organized. The writers set out to explain why they endorse *S* by presenting reasons for *S*. In discussing each of these reasons in turn, they attempt to accomplish what they set out to do, to explain in some detail why they endorse *S*. If they do this with persuasive evidence and reasoning, they may even persuade us to believe *S*. If they fail to persuade us, at least they have done us the intellectual courtesy of explaining why they believe *S*, and we can now argue with them, if we are so minded. Another way of explaining this kind of organization is as follows: The writer sets up a series of targets (*l . . . n*) so that he knows precisely what is required of him in the body of the theme. When he has accomplished this, he is finished. Since the theme is short, no summary or conclusion is required.

Length and Scope of Themes

Impromptu themes run from 300 to 400 words. Since the reasons, whatever their emotional value, are of equivalent intellectual value, it follows that theoretically the same number of words should be devoted to the discussion of each (in the case of three reasons and 400 words, about 133 words to each paragraph). In actual practice, of course, this is not done for the obvious reason that evidence and reasoning are not measured by word-counts. A short paragraph may at times prove more persuasive than a long paragraph. But the fact that time limits us to about 400 words means that we need to restrict our reasons to two or three major ones, and that these two or three reasons should represent units of thought that can be supported with evidence and reasoning. If we have too many reasons, or if the few reasons we have chosen represent excessively large units of thought, we shall be forced either to treat them superficially or to treat one reason thoroughly at the expense of the others. Given a limited scope, then, of about 400 words, the principle to remember is that the more ground we attempt to cover in themes, the less deeply we shall be able to explore our reasons. Conversely, the more deeply we explore our reasons, the less ground we shall be able to cover.

When a reason represents too large a unit of thought—too large a *subset*—we can always divide the subset into more manageable subsets, as explained below.

Dividing Subsets into More Manageable Subsets

Suppose you are assigned to write a 400-word theme on the topic, "Your opinion concerning obscenity laws." Suppose too that after some deliberation you develop the following thesis sentence: "The Supreme Court should eliminate obscenity laws because such laws vary from county to county, infringe upon civil liberties, and restrain free trade." Upon inspection you find that your thesis sentence is satisfactory in every respect except *scope*; for you realize that the thesis sentence, as it stands, is going to force you to cover too much ground and to be superficial. Upon further inspection you see that all of your subsets can be divided as specified below. And you see too that each of your original subsets contains within it the basis for a theme that is sufficiently limited in scope for a 400-word theme.

Subset 1
. . . such laws vary so much from county to county

Subset 1 Divided
. . . such laws vary from county to county in definition, enforcement, and penalties.

Subset 2
. . . infringe upon civil liberties

Subset 2 Divided
. . . they infringe upon free speech, inhibit the creation of artistic works, and dictate what people can read and see.

Subset 3
. . . restrain free trade

Subset 3 Divided
. . . they restrain censored works from being produced and distributed, reduce the employment force involved in their production and distribution, and force up prices on those works.

Given these divisions of your original subsets, you now have three thesis sentences that read as follows:

1. The Supreme Court should eliminate obscenity laws because such laws vary from county to county in definition, enforcement, and penalties.
2. The Supreme Court should eliminate obscenity laws because they infringe upon free speech, inhibit the creation of artistic works, and dictate what people can read and see.
3. The Supreme Court should eliminate obscenity laws because they restrain censored works from being produced and distributed, reduce the employment force involved in their production and distribution, and force up prices on those works.

Exercises M

1. Which of the following thesis sentences can be most adequately developed in a 400-word theme?
   a. By and large, college professors are becoming less and less secure in their positions because of the introduction of many new teaching devices, because universities are turning out larger and larger numbers of Ph.D.'s, and because the curriculum throughout the United States is becoming more and more uniform.

b. Pesticides should be outlawed because they disturb the balance of nature and poison food products.

c. Lobbying should be outlawed because lobbyists put undue pressure on legislators and try to make the law serve their special-interest groups.

d. TV commercials should be regulated to see that they do not misrepresent their products and that they are not offensive to public taste.

2. How would you divide the first subset in *a* above ("introduction of new teaching devices") so that you could write adequately upon it in a 400-word theme?

3. Write a 400-word theme outside of class. Apply in this theme everything you have learned about thesis-sentence organization. The subject may be your own or one assigned by your instructor. Suggested topics follow.

Suggested WHY Topics

1. Should the sale of firearms be prohibited?
2. Should college admissions be determined by race or sex quotas?
3. Should a person's past sexual history be admissible evidence in a rape case?
4. Should students receive course credit for *x* activity?
5. What I regard as a student's rights.
6. Why I would advocate (not advocate) National Health Insurance.
7. Should students' evaluations play a role in the promotion and tenure of teachers?
8. Why I think the murder of Martin Luther King, Jr. (John F. Kennedy) was the result of a conspiracy.
9. Why many high school students graduate uneducated.
10. Why students should (should not) work their way through college.
11. Why students should (should not) engage in extracurricular activities.
12. Should class attendance be voluntary in college?
13. Should final examinations be abolished in college?
14. Should conference athletics be abolished?
15. Should students marry while in college?
16. Is an honor system practicable in my college?
17. Should all students be allowed to have cars on campus?
18. Should entrance examinations be made more stringent at my college?
19. Should my college introduce entrance examinations?
20. Should grading at my college be only pass/fail?
21. Should liquor be allowed on campus?
22. Should students be required to live in supervised housing?
23. Should standards for the driver's license be raised in my state?
24. Is watching soap operas a waste of time?
25. Should communists be allowed to teach in college?
26. Should the draft be reinstituted in the United States?
27. Should price supports for tobacco be continued?
28. Should there be price controls for the oil industry?
29. Should American citizens be guaranteed a minimum income?
30. Is a volunteer army good or bad?

31. Should strikes by public employees be outlawed?
32. Should lobbying be outlawed?
33. Should books (movies, magazines, TV, etc.) be censored?
34. Should the federal government require automobile manufacturers to equip all new cars with all known safety devices?
35. Should the United States have withdrawn from Vietnam?
36. Should there be unconditional amnesty for American soldiers who deserted during the Vietnam War?
37. Should the electoral college be abandoned?
38. Should the CIA be abolished?
39. Should Richard M. Nixon have resigned the presidency?
40. Should marijuana (prostitution, gambling, etc.) be legalized?

2 **What** Topics

We said that all theme and essay topics are of two basic kinds: *why* topics and *what* topics. In some ways these two kinds of topics have much in common; in other ways they have very little in common. Below appear examples of *what* and *why* topics. What does your examination of them reveal?

**Examples A:
WHAT and WHY
Topics**

WHAT Topics	WHY Topics
1. Contrast the gun laws of two states	1. Should gun laws be tightened in the United States?
2. Discuss some major geological formations of the Grand Canyon	2. Should the Grand Canyon be closed to campers?
3. What are some of the extracurricular activities offered at your college?	3. Should freshmen students engage in extracurricular activities?
4. Discuss the origin, purpose, and function of the Electoral College	4. Should the Electoral College be abolished?
5. Discuss the varieties of final examinations given at your college	5. Should the final-examination system be abolished at my college?
6. Discuss some leading characteristics of T. S. Eliot's poetry.	6. Is T. S. Eliot a major poet?
7. The public arguments in favor of (in opposition to) nuclear power stations*	7. Are nuclear power stations dangerous?

The main thing that your examination of these topics should have revealed is that *what* topics call for **information only**, whereas *why* topics call for **opinion plus information**. For instance, the first *what* topic above ("Contrast the gun laws of two states") would be answered by a **thesis sentence** like this:

* As was pointed out in the footnote on page 4, the views, arguments, and opinions of others belong to the class of facts, so long as we do not distort them. It is a fact that some people have the opinion that no man walked on the moon and that the feat was only a television stunt. Even though this opinion is held is disregard of the facts, it nevertheless remains a fact that some people have the opinion that the moon walks were television stunts.

"The extreme variation in gun laws in the United States can be seen by examining gun laws of New York (a state with severe gun regulations) and Texas (a state with lax gun regulations)." However, the first *why* topic above ("Should gun laws be tightened in the United States?") would be answered in one of the following ways:

Positive:
Gun laws should be tightened because statistics show that states with stringent gun laws have lower murder rates than those with lax gun laws and that killers are most frequently ordinary armed citizens, not armed gangsters.

Negative:
Gun laws should be liberalized in all states because citizens have a Constitutional right to protect their country against attack and to defend their homes from intruders.

If you now reexamine the three thesis sentences on gun laws we just presented, you will see that the elements of a *why* set are **reasons**, whereas the elements of a *what* set consist of **information**.* Thus, with *why* topics, we have to arrive at opinions; with *what* topics, opinions are entirely out of the question, for we are concerned only with information.

Exercise A:
Distinguishing WHAT
and WHY Topics

Examine the topics below and determine which are *what* topics and which *why* topics. Provide a basis for your judgments.

1. Major tenets of John Calvin's theology
2. Kinds of thinking
3. The case for (or against) unionizing the United States Army
4. Should marijuana be sold in tobacco shops?
5. The Catholic sacraments
6. Should lobbying be prohibited by law?
7. A report on the lobbying activities of the National Rifle Association
8. Public opinions concerning violence on TV
9. The uses of radioisotopes

The thesis sentence we write for *what* topics resembles the thesis sentence we write for *why* topics, especially as regards *parallelism* (grammatical and logical) and *relevance* (see pages 10–13). The key difference, then, between the two kinds of thesis sentences is in *purpose*. The purpose of a *why* thesis sentence is (1) to identify our opinion of a topic and (2) to specify our reasons for holding that opinion (the reasons that we intend to discuss in the theme). The purpose of a *what* thesis sentence is (1) to identify our topic and (2) to specify the facts of that topic (the facts that we intend to explain in the theme). Examples of *what* thesis sentences appear below.

*To simplify discussion, we shall henceforth refer to elements and subsets, which are collections of elements, simply as elements, though this is taking mathematical liberty with the terms.

Examples B: **Thesis Sentences for** **WHAT Topics**	**WHAT Topics**	**Thesis Sentences Drawn from WHAT Topics**
	1. Major tenets of John Calvin's theology	1. Three major tenets of John Calvin's theology are total depravity, unconditional election, and perseverance of saints.
	2. Kinds of thinking	2. Four major kinds of thinking are reverie, decision-making, rationalization, and creative thought.*
	3. The Catholic sacraments	3. The seven Catholic sacraments are baptism, communion, confirmation, marriage, orders, penance, and unction.

Inasmuch as the *what* and *why* thesis sentences are so radically different in purpose, we need to distinguish one from the other. Symbols again prove very convenient.

The *l . . . n* of the *what* thesis sentence do not, as we said, designate *reasons* for affirming or denying *S*. Instead, *l . . . n* designate the *facts* of *S*. Therefore, we need new symbols to designate the elements of a *what* thesis sentence. Since we have already used the numerical series to designate the elements of a *why* thesis sentence, we shall now use the alphabetical series (*a, b . . . v*) to designate the elements of a *what* thesis sentence. (The letter *v* is the symbol for *variable* and is to the alphabetical series what *n* is to the numerical series, an unspecified number of elements). Thus, if we reduce *why* and *what* thesis sentences to more or less symbolic formulations, they read as follows:

WHY thesis sentence: S because of *l . . . n*
WHAT thesis sentence: S contains *a . . . v*

Exercises B

1. In *Examples B* above appear three *what* thesis sentences. Copy them on theme paper and underline *S* twice and *a . . . v* once. (Do not underline the linking words *are* and *and*.)
2. Suppose you were reading a theme on the topic, "A sample of student answers to questions about Grand Canyon National Park" and encountered the statements below. Which of them would you identify as *fact* (never mind if they falsify fact) and which as *opinion* (never mind if you agree with the opinion)?
   a. Grand Canyon National Park is located in northwestern Arizona and covers an area of more than one thousand square miles.
   b. Ten of one hundred persons interviewed on this campus did not know the location of Grand Canyon National Park; thirty-five of them refused to hazard a guess about its magnitude.

*This thesis sentence is drawn from James Harvey Robinson's essay "On Various Kinds of Thinking" in *The Mind in the Making* (New York: Harper & Brothers, 1921), pp. 33–62.

    c. One of the persons interviewed thought the Grand Canyon was a crater on the moon.

    d. The Grand Canyon of the Arkansas is the Royal Gorge, a canyon with one-thousand-foot walls.

    e. The number of people allowed into Grand Canyon National Park should be reduced so as to reduce pollution.

3. Write two *what* thesis sentences of your own and title them: Two *What* Thesis Sentences.

In discussing sets earlier (pages 7–9), we made the point that some sets are limited and easily exhausted, but that other sets, for all practical purposes, are inexhaustible. The thesis sentence, then, takes one of two forms, depending upon whether the elements of the set can be easily exhausted or whether they can be only represented:

S is representable by elements *a . . . v*

S is exhausted by elements *a . . . v*

The analyses below of two thesis sentences we have already considered make the point clearer.

a, *b*, *c* are elements of the large set "The tenets of John Calvin's theology" and only *represent* the set rather than exhaust it.	*S* Three major tenets of John Calvin's theology *a* total depravity *b* unconditional election *c* perseverance of saints
a, *b*, *c*, *d*, *e*, *f*, *g* are elements of the set "The seven Catholic sacraments" and *exhaust* the set rather than only represent it.	*S* The seven Catholic sacraments *a* baptism *b* communion *c* confirmation *d* marriage *e* orders *f* penance *g* unction

---

Definition of Trivial and Nontrivial Thesis Sentences for WHAT Topics

On pages 6–7, we explained how a writer can trivialize a *why* topic by offering nothing persuasive in the way of evidence, reasoning, and point of view. Such trivialization, we also said, is sometimes the result of choosing what for the writer is an inauthentic subject, one about which he feels and knows little. The situation is somewhat different for *what* topics (though obviously the writer needs to choose topics that are authentic for him) for the reason that *what* topics have a different purpose from *why* topics. Thus, a thesis sentence for a *what* topic is considered significant (nontrivial) when *S or* its elements or both are so little known to one's audience as to require reasonably full explanation. Conversely, a thesis sentence for a *what* topic is considered trivial when both *S and* its elements are too familiar to require much elaboration.

Exercises C   1. Sort out the nontrivial and trivial thesis sentences in the examples below.
                                       Provide the reason for your judgments.
                                       a. A baseball team consists of nine players—three outfielders, three base-
                                          men, a shortstop, a pitcher, and a catcher.
                                       b. Three features of modern poetry are synesthesia, the merging of sound
                                          and sense, and private images.
                                       c. My wardrobe consists of four suits, two jackets, three sweaters, fifteen
                                          shirts, eight ties, fourteen hankerchiefs, two belts, one pair of sus-
                                          penders, ten pairs of socks, and two pairs of shoes.
                                       d. Some major measures passed under President Lyndon B. Johnson's
                                          administration are Medicare for the Aged, the Voting Rights Bill, and War
                                          on Poverty.
                                       e. The three dramatic unities are time, place, and action.
                                    2. On theme paper write two thesis sentences for *what* topics, one that rep-
                                       resents *S*, another that exhausts *S*. Be sure your thesis sentences are non-
                                       trivial.

Organizing the Whole Theme

As with the numerical series of the *why* thesis sentence, the alphabetical series
(*a . . . v*) designates not only the elements of *S* but also the *order* in which
those elements are to be arranged in the thesis sentence and discussed in the
theme. Again one must choose the order that is most logical in the circumstances. The choices here are limited to six: (1) *random arrangement*, (2)
partially random arrangement, (3) *nonrandom arrangement*, (4) *climactic arrangement*, (5) *chronological arrangement*, and (6) *partially chronological
arrangement*.

Random arrangement may be used when no one of the elements has more
value than any other, or when no one of them is necessary to an understanding
of another. For example, we may arrange the elements in the following set in
any way we like: "Three common misconceptions about Catholics are that
they worship the Pope, they hate Protestants, and they reject birth control."

Partially random arrangement, a variation of *simple-to-complex arrangement*
(see page 14) should be used when one or more but not all of the elements
have to be so positioned in the series as to make the other elements easier
for the writer to explain and the reader to understand. In the following example, for instance, we may arrange any of the elements except the last in any
order we wish: "TV commercials occur in the form of testimonials, musicals,
demonstrations, short lectures, graphics, or in some combination of these."

Nonrandom arrangement should be used when a discussion of one element
makes it easier for the writer to explain and for the reader to grasp a second
element, and so on. For example, if the doctrine of total depravity is explained
first, a second doctrine—unconditional election—becomes easier to discuss
and to understand. Similarly, a discussion of unconditional election makes the
explanation of a third doctrine—the perseverance of saints—simpler to discuss
as well as to grasp. (See "Three Major Tenets of John Calvin's Theology,"
pages 43–44.)

Climactic arrangement should be observed when *a . . . v* call for an ordering of value. Consider this thesis sentence, for instance: "Four major kinds of thinking are reverie, decision-making, rationalization, and creative thought." As *thought*, "reverie" clearly has less value than "decision-making"; "decision-making" (as James Harvey Robinson defines the term) has less value than "rationalization"; and "creative thought" has more value than any of the other elements.

Chronological arrangement is called for when the events to be discussed occurred in a certain clear-cut time sequence, as in the thesis sentence: "The countries that have influenced Cuban history are Spain, the United States, and the Soviet Union."

Partially chronological arrangement should be used when one or more but not all of the elements fit a time sequence. Among the elements of "the seven Catholic sacraments," baptism clearly precedes confirmation in point of time, and confirmation precedes marriage (if one marries) or orders (if one decides to become a priest), and all these precede unction. Communion and penance, however, are not sacraments that are conferred once and once only; they cannot, therefore, be fitted into a chronological pattern. In such instances, only a partially chronological arrangement can be used.

Once the *order* of the elements is determined in the thesis sentence, the *arrangement* of them in the body of the theme becomes self-evident. Thus, since the thesis sentence itself is the first paragraph of the theme, *a* will be discussed in the second paragraph, *b* in the third, *c* in the fourth, etc.

Below appear two student themes developed from two of the thesis sentences we have already examined. The first theme discusses representative elements of *S*; the second theme exhausts the elements of *S*.

Themes Exemplifying Thesis Sentence Organization of WHAT Topics

THREE MAJOR TENETS OF JOHN CALVIN'S THEOLOGY*

Three major tenets of John Calvin's theology as found in his *Institutes of the Christian Religion* (first published in 1536) are total depravity, unconditional election, and the perseverance of saints.

The doctrine of total depravity is the belief that man is evil by nature because he inherits the corruption of Adam when he fell from grace (see Genesis). As the *New England Primer* has it, "In Adam's Fall/We sinned all." This being the case, man is helpless to achieve grace or salvation, whether by faith or good works or both. In fact, according to this doctrine, man deserves to suffer eternal perdition because, given his inherent corruption, he is the creator of evil in a world that God created free of evil.

The doctrine of unconditional election is evidence of God's mercy. For

*This student theme is based upon Rod W. Horton and Herbert W. Edwards, *Backgrounds of American Literary Thought*, 2d ed. (New York: Appleton-Century-Crofts, 1967), pp. 20–21; the King James Version of the Bible; *Encyclopaedia Britannica* (1961); Wilhelm Niesel, *The Theology of Calvin*, translated by Harold Knight (London: Lutterworth Press, 1956); and James D. Hart, *Oxford Companion to American Literature* (New York: Oxford University Press, 1956), p. 112.

despite man's corrupt nature, God saves (elects) a number of us. The key text here is Romans 9:18—"Therefore hath he mercy on whom he will *have mercy*, and whom he will, he hardeneth." As was said earlier, none of us can earn grace; it is a gift conferred upon some of us by God. To beseech God for grace by prayer or attempt to earn grace by faith and good works cannot alter His divine decision. In the words of Alexander Pope's *Essay on Man*: "Think we, like some weak prince, the Eternal Cause/Prone for his favourites to reverse his laws?/ . . . When the loose mountain trembles from on high,/Shall gravitation cease, if you go by?" God's judgment, then, is as irreversible as the law of gravitation.

The doctrine of the perseverance of saints (the elect) follows logically from the doctrine of unconditional election. God being omnipotent, none can resist His divine gift of election. This doctrine also advances the belief that those who are granted grace are exempted from further evil-doing and, to that extent, become deserving of salvation—not, it should be stressed again, by their own decision, but by God's.

THE SEVEN CATHOLIC SACRAMENTS*

The seven sacraments of the Roman Catholic and Greek Catholic churches are baptism, communion, confirmation, marriage, orders, penance, and unction.

Baptism serves to clean away all previous and original sin and to initiate one into the body of Christ, namely, the church. Biblical support for baptism derives from Mark 1:9: "And it came to pass in those days, that Jesus came from Nazareth of Galilee, and was baptized of John in Jordan," for "John did . . . preach the baptism of repentance for the remission of sins" (1:4). Except for the Society of Friends (Quakers) and the Salvation Army, which recognize no sacraments at all, all Protestant sects hold baptism to be a sacrament. The procedure of baptism varies, of course, from the sprinkling of holy water (Catholic) to total immersion (Baptist). A further variation is that Catholics generally baptize children, whereas Baptists and some other sects baptize only those who have reached the age of decision, usually adolescence or adulthood.

Perhaps the most sacred of all the sacraments is that which Protestants call Holy Communion and that which Roman Catholics call Holy Eucharist. This sacrament reenacts a key event in Jesus' life and commemorates His death upon the cross "for many for the remission of sins." The biblical basis for this sacrament is Matthew 26:26–28 (a portion of which has just been quoted). Breaking bread at the Last Supper, Jesus "blessed it . . . and gave it to the disciples, and said, Take, eat; this is my body." And taking up the cup of wine, He "gave it to them, saying, Drink ye all of it; For this is my blood of the new testament. . . ." In all Protestant churches the communion service is symbolic, the bread or wafer representing Christ's body and the wine or grape juice representing His blood. To Catholics, however, the elements actually become the body and blood of Christ, transubstantiated by the priest. The significance

*This student theme is based upon articles in *Encyclopaedia Britannica* (1961); *Encyclopedia Americana* (1963); *Collier's Encyclopedia* (1952); *Universal Standard Encyclopedia* (1955); *Encyclopaedia of Religion and Ethics*, edited by James Hastings (1926); and *Life* 41 (December 17, 1956), pp. 75–85; as well as upon the King James Version of the Bible.

of this sacrament, however administered, is that the worshipper partakes of Christ in some form and his soul is thereby nourished for eternal life.

The sacrament of confirmation completes the work of baptism by making one a communicant of the church. This sacrament is bestowed upon a person some time between his seventh and fourteenth year. Its biblical basis is Acts 8:14–17, which describes how Peter and John "laid their hands" upon the Samaritans so that "They received the Holy Ghost."

Marriage is also held to be a sacrament by Catholics, whether Roman or Greek, though Protestants consider it a ceremony or rite. In support of their belief that Christ intended matrimony to be a sacrament, Catholics point to His presence at the "marriage in Cana of Galilee" where He performed His first miracle, the changing of water into wine (John 2:1–11). This sacrament sanctifies human life, procreation, and the religious, as well as the secular, education of children. For this reason Catholics oppose divorce, though they are prepared to annul any marriage when it can be proved to have been invalid from the start.

Orders or ordination is another of the sacraments of the Roman Catholic and Greek Catholic Churches. When a bishop ordains a man as a minister of God, he continues a process initiated by Jesus who told His apostles: ". . . as my Father hath sent me, even so send I you. And when he had said this, he breathed on them, and saith unto them, Receive ye the Holy Ghost . . ." (John 20:21–22). His apostles, in turn, chose others to ordain and this continues the tradition known as the apostolic succession. At a crucial moment in the ordination procedure, the bishop places his hands on the head of the candidate and confers upon him the authority of a priest.

The sacrament of penance is one of mercy. The Catholic confesses his sins and is granted absolution or forgiveness. Roman Catholics confess privately to a priest in a confession box; Greek Orthodox Catholics confess individually to the priest before the altar. Such confessions are, of course, privileged. Devout Catholics confess as often as once a week and are, according to the degree of their sins, required to perform penance, either the saying of extra prayers or the payment of contributions to the church. Some Protestant sects, like the Episcopalians, confess as a group; still other sects espouse the doctrine of the priesthood of all believers, feeling that anyone of their religious persuasion may be a "father confessor." There are several texts in the New Testament that serve as a basis for this sacrament, perhaps the most important being John 20:23. When Christ returned to His disciples after His resurrection, He said, "Whose soever sins ye remit, they are remitted unto them; and whose soever sins ye retain, they are retained."

The basis for the seventh sacrament is the Epistle of St. James the Apostle (5:14–15): "Is any sick among you? let him call for the elders of the church; and let them pray over him, anointing him with oil in the name of the Lord: And the prayer of faith shall save the sick, and the Lord shall raise him up; and if he have committed sins, they shall be forgiven him." Greek Orthodox Catholics, like a wing in the Episcopal Church, administer unction in times of sickness. Roman Catholics, however, administer unction only when death is imminent to assure the soul of grace during its final moments on earth; hence, the term *extreme unction*. In theory, the individual must begin this sacrament by confessing his sins, but this requirement is ordinarily waived.

Exercise D

Write a 400- to 500-word theme outside of class, applying all that you have learned about *what* topics. Suggested topics appear below.

Once you contemplate your topic, you will feel the force of the point that *what* topics call for answers largely in the public domain. You will, therefore, need to consult appropriate sources of information either in person (as in interviews), or in print, or both, before you formulate your thesis sentence. To avoid the charge of plagiarism* (1) use no fewer than three sources of information, (2) make sure that you acknowledge those sources in your theme, and (3) report your findings in your own words. Be sure to revise your theme as many times as necessary to achieve perfect organization and flawless mechanics.

Suggested WHAT Topics

1. Historians' views of the causes of the American Revolution (French Revolution, American Civil War, Russian Revolution, Cuban Revolution, Portuguese Revolution, etc.)
2. Some forms of church worship
3. Some forms of church government
4. Some features of propaganda
5. Misconceptions about a minority group
6. Kinds of maps
7. Kinds of prisons in the United States
8. What Hindus (Buddhists, Confucianists, Taoists, Moslems, etc.) believe
9. Chief Antarctic expeditions
10. Major discoveries in atomic research
11. The blood types
12. Purposes of the United Nations

*Plagiarism is the cardinal crime in the academic world and must be avoided at all cost. Plagiarism is defined as the attempt to fob off another's thought or language as one's own, whether throughout an entire paper or in any portion of a paper. Whether one steals from published or unpublished sources or has someone else write his paper for him, the offense is equally great. There is never a need to plagiarize, and, when plagiarism is committed, it is usually done out of ignorance of the rules. No one, especially your instructor, expects you to have a boundless store of information. Even seasoned scholars have to consult printed materials to check the accuracy of their information or to gain fresh information, and you are not only equally entitled to this privilege but are heartily encouraged to exercise it. The only rules to follow to avoid the charge of plagiarism are these: (1) If you borrow from an author, whether that borrowing represents an idea, a judgment, or uncommon information, and you put that borrowing into your own words, simply acknowledge the source, either in your text or in a footnote; (2) if you borrow from an author *together with his language*, put that borrowing into quotation marks and acknowledge the source, either in your text or in a footnote. If the information you borrow is common knowledge, such as the dates of the battles of the Civil War, you need make no acknowledgment at all. If, however, the information you borrow is uncommon (that Horace Greeley, for example, agitating for a quick victory in his *New York Tribune*, "did much to drive the Federal government into the precipitate action that culminated in the disaster at Bull Run"), acknowledge the source, in this case Gerald W. Johnson, *The Lunatic Fringe* (Philadelphia and New York: J. B. Lippincott Co., 1957), pp. 70–71.

13. What Indians think of life on a reservation
14. Ways of testing soil
15. The six simple machines
16. Some famous American (English, German, French, etc.) landmarks
17. The uses of radioisotopes
18. Sociologists' views of the causes of juvenile delinquency
19. Kinds of law courts in the United States
20. Key features of modern painting (music, literature, architecture, dance, etc.)
21. Types of reformers
22. Theories about the origin of our solar system
23. Theories about the Ice Ages
24. Kinds of banks in the United States
25. Mythical animals
26. The Crusades
27. The causes of tides
28. Major kinds of alphabets
29. Kinds of jobs for graduates in English (agriculture, economics, geography, etc.)
30. Kinds of marriage institutions
31. The causes of volcanoes
32. Ways in which mountains are formed
33. The successive discoveries of America
34. Main causes of automobile accidents
35. The public arguments favoring (opposing) collective bargaining for teachers
36. The public arguments against (in favor of) National Health Insurance
37. How shoplifters are treated in my county
38. The major beliefs of a church
39. Some schools of psychology (sociology, history, economics, etc.)
40. Some characteristics of Emily Dickinson's poetry (or Robert Frost's, William Butler Yeats's, etc.)

3 How Topics

Except for three crucial differences, *how* topics are almost exactly like *what* topics, which is precisely what we might expect, since *how* topics are only a permutation of *what* topics. One key thing they have in common is that they both call for informational answers. The topic, "How Louis Pasteur discovered the principle of vaccination," or "How Thomas Paine's bones disappeared," can be legitimately rephrased as follows: "What happened that enabled Louis Pasteur to discover the principle of vaccination?" and "What circumstances led to the disappearance of Thomas Paine's bones?"

Exercises A   Convert the *how* topics below into *what* topics.

1. How Troy was rediscovered
2. How an electric eye works
3. How Anton van Leeuwenhoek invented the microscope
4. How George Washington won the victory at Trenton
5. How to make pottery on a wheel
6. How to cultivate pearls
7. How Siamese twins are separated
8. How X-rays are taken
9. How to make hydrochloric acid
10. How Thomas Alva Edison invented the phonograph

Despite the fact that *how* topics can be converted into *what* topics, *what* topics cannot be converted into *how* topics. Sometimes, of course, a *what* topic will masquerade as a *how* topic (e.g., "*How* the United States Congress is organized"), a fact which should remind us that one cannot depend upon the mere occurrence of the words *what* and *how* in the topic to tell us what the topic is asking us to do.

Exercises B   Attempt to convert the *what* topics below into *how* topics. What conclusion do you draw from your effort?

1. What are the purposes of the United Nations?
2. What are some customs of the Navaho Indians?
3. What are some modern personality theories?
4. What are some characteristic themes of William Faulkner's fiction?
5. What were the purposes of the latest American space flight?

The *how* topic is a set, just as the *what* topic is a set. Moreover, both *what* and *how* topics are sets of facts, which is to say that the answers to them are to be found in print—in books, magazines, newspapers, and pamphlets—or in interviews with authorities in the field, unless, of course, one has already absorbed the pertinent information. Too, the thesis sentence (*S* contains *a . . . v*) is used to organize the information to be presented.

Examples A:
Thesis Sentences for
HOW Topics

1. Kokichi Mikimoto cultivated pearls by introducing an irritant into the oyster and waiting from three to ten years until the nacre (mother-of-pearl) was formed.
2. To put on a dress shirt, slip your arms through the sleeves, button the shirt, and tuck the tail into your trousers.
3. To order a book, go to your local bookstore and give the clerk the necessary information about the book (title, author, and publisher).
4. To separate Siamese twins, surgeons have to cut through the bone that connects the two, clamp the blood vessels that they share, and then rebuild the tissue exposed by surgery.

Notice that the thesis sentences above observe the principles of relevance and parallelism, as all thesis sentences should. But notice too that some of these thesis sentences are trivial. The definition for nontrivial *how* topics is the same as for *what* topics: *S* is nontrivial when *S* or its elements or both are so little known as to require reasonably full explanation.

Exercise C

Which of the thesis sentences in *Examples A* above seem trivial? Which nontrivial? Explain. (For purposes of this exercise, ignore the possibility that an author such as James Thurber might write a highly amusing essay on such a trivial-seeming topic as "How to put on an overcoat.")

The Three Major Differences Between WHAT and HOW Topics

The three major differences between *what* and *how* topics are these. First, a *how* topic is a description of (1) a process (how something works or worked), (2) a procedure (how something is or was done), or (3) an event (how something occurred or is occurring). For example, the topic "How an airplane works" calls for the description of a process; "How the first heart transplant operation was performed" calls for the description of a procedure; "The stages in putting a man on the moon" calls for an exposition of the sequence by which a man was finally landed on Earth's satellite.

Secondly, one can seldom generalize upon the findings of a *how* topic. The way, for instance, airplanes work today is not necessarily the way they worked when the Wright brothers first flew their plane at Kitty Hawk in 1903, nor the way they may work in the future. Similarly, the way the first heart transplant operation was performed by Dr. Christiaan N. Barnard in South Africa in 1967 is not necessarily the way the operation is performed today or may be performed in the future. Likewise, the way Neil Armstrong was landed on the moon in 1969 is not necessarily the way a person may be landed on a more distant satellite in the future.

The third major difference between *how* and *what* topics is this: in discussing a *how* topic, we have no choice about arranging the elements of the set in the thesis sentence or, therefore, in the successive paragraphs of our theme. The reason for this is that the elements in a *how* set are certain distinctly consecutive and intimately linked steps that admit of one and only one arrangement—a presentation of the elements in which they occur or have occurred. To explain: If we trace the steps that led Louis Pasteur to discover the vaccination principle (as is done on pages 34–35), we shall find that the elements must be arranged in the following order: (a) his work with "diseased" wine; (b) his work with diseased silkworms; (c) his work with diseased chickens; (d) his work with diseased sheep; and (e) his work with diseased people. No step in this process may be omitted, though it may be summarized, and no arrangement other than a strictly consecutive one may be used.

To take another example: The topic "How Thomas Paine's bones disappeared" calls for two steps, neither of which may be omitted and both of which must be presented in consecutive order, as in the specimen theme below.

Exercises D

1. In what ways is a *how* topic like a *what* topic?
2. In what three crucial ways does a *how* topic differ from a *what* topic?
3. Write two *how* topics of your own and cast each of them into a thesis sentence that is nontrivial and that observes the principles of parallelism and relevance.
4. Below appear two student themes that develop a *how* topic. After you examine them carefully, write a 400- to 500-word theme on a *how* topic. Suggested topics appear at the end of this chapter. To avoid such trivial topics as "How I get up in the morning," you will want to consult appropriate sources of information and take notes on your findings before you write your theme. To avoid the charge of plagiarism, (1) use no fewer than three sources of information, (2) report your findings in your own words, (3) identify your sources in your theme, and (4) review the footnote about plagiarism on page 29. Be sure to revise your theme as often as necessary to achieve perfect organization and flawless mechanics.

Themes Exemplifying Thesis-Sentence Organization of HOW Topics

HOW THOMAS PAINE'S BONES DISAPPEARED*

The two main links in the chain of circumstances that led to the disappearance of Thomas Paine's bones are the American reception of his book *The Age of Reason* and the harebrained scheme of William Cobbett.

Paine's extremely deistic work, *The Age of Reason* (Part I, 1794; Part II, 1795),

*This student theme is based upon information in Frank Smith, *Thomas Paine: Liberator* (New York: Frederick A. Stokes Co., 1938); Leo Gurko, *Tom Paine: Freedom's Apostle* (New York: Thomas Y. Crowell Co., 1957); and upon Thomas Paine, "From *The Age of Reason*," in Walter Blair, Theodore Hornberger, and Randall Stewart, eds., *The Literature of the United States* (Chicago: Scott, Foresman & Co., 1953), 1: 282–84, 358–65.

a section of which was written while he was interned in a French prison, shocked the American masses, who probably only heard preachers denounce it from the pulpit or who read only lurid newspaper accounts of its blasphemy —its denial of the Trinity, its claim that the Bible was so much mythology, and its charge that the church was an instrument of terror and extortion. His name came to stand for atheism, despite the fact that he affirmed the existence of God and argued that God manifested Himself presently and continuously through nature and nature's laws, not only on past occasions through special revelations and through special "vessels." "His English publisher," as Blair, Hornberger, and Stewart tell us, "was prosecuted for blasphemy"; there was a movement afoot "to burn Paine at the stake"; and when he was finally released from prison and returned in 1802 to the America he had helped to free, he was—to quote Blair et al. again—"shot at through his window, insulted in the streets, and humiliated on his deathbed by clergymen" who sought to wring from him a last-minute confession, not to mention that he was widely defamed after his death.

Knowing in advance that no religious sect would give his remains rest in their cemeteries, he nevertheless hoped that the Quakers might relent in the end, for he was a Quaker himself. When upon his death the Quakers refused him burial, he was interred on his New Rochelle farm, the farm in New York that had been given him for his extraordinary services as the Winston Churchill of the American Revolution. But his bones were to find no permanent haven there. A decade after his burial, William Cobbett, an eccentric English revolutionary who lived in America at times, conceived the ghoulish notion that he would disinter Paine's bones, take them to England, and "exhibit them as part of a scheme to reform society there," to use the words of Blair et al. again. Though Cobbett succeeded in his ghoulishness, English law enforcers prevented him from exhibiting Paine's bones and they were stored away. According to legend, Cobbett's son received the bones as part of his legacy. When he fell into debt, he auctioned Paine's bones to pay his creditors. At this point in their wild career, the bones of Paine vanished, and to this day no one knows where they are.

HOW LOUIS PASTEUR DISCOVERED THE PRINCIPLE OF VACCINATION*

Louis Pasteur discovered the principle of vaccination by investigating the reasons for wine's souring and then applying what he had learned to silkworms, to domestic animals, and finally to man.

Pasteur was a practicing chemist when spoiled wine created a serious economic problem in France. In "healthy" wines the grape juice simply fermented to produce alcohol, whereas "sick" wines became gluey and vinegary. Applying himself to the problem, Pasteur found that "healthy" fermentation is due to the action of yeast (a mass of fungi) and that "unhealthy" fermentation is due to the action of bacteria. To prove his theory, he filled two flasks with the identical solution and boiled them both. Then he sealed the first flask to prevent bacteria from entering the solution, but left the second flask exposed to the air. Allowing time for fermentation to occur, he found that the sealed

*This student theme is based upon material in *Collier's Encyclopedia* (1952); *Encyclopedia Americana* (1963); *Encyclopaedia Britannica* (1961); and Howard W. Haggard, *Devils, Drugs and Doctors* (New York: Harper & Brothers, 1929).

flask contained "healthy" wine and the exposed flask "sick" wine. The solution that Pasteur proposed, in the light of his findings, was that wine should be heated and sealed. This process of heating a liquid to the point where germs are destroyed without doing damage to the fluid is called pasteurization, and it has been applied not only to wines but to milk as well, which used to be a chief breeding-ground for such germs as those that produce tuberculosis and typhoid.

Having solved this problem, Pasteur turned to another one—the diseases afflicting silkworms—that, economically, was far more critical, for it affected not only France, a leading producer of silk, but other silk-producing countries as well. His solution this time did not occur with dramatic suddenness. In fact, he arrived at a solution only after five years of study, for the problem was more complicated. He discovered that the silkworms were suffering, not from one but two infectious diseases; but he finally provided preventatives for both diseases and thus restored prosperity to the silk industry.

His next problem began with a study of contagious diseases among domestic animals. While making this study Pasteur chanced upon the only accidental discovery of his career, but one that turned out to be his most important. He had been doing research on chicken cholera, a highly contagious disease, and he had isolated the bacillus and was growing it in a broth culture. To maintain the colony, he found it necessary to add fresh broth fairly often, else the bacilli would poison themselves with their own waste products. Pasteur, therefore, freshened the cultures by taking a small amount of the broth containing the bacilli and putting it in fresh broth. Whenever he fed this broth to chickens, they unfailingly died of cholera. One day, quite by accident, he chanced to feed chickens with bacilli that had grown in a culture to which no fresh broth had been recently added. Instead of dying, these chickens only became sick for a few days and recovered: The bacteria had become weakened and were less virulent in the "old" broth than they were in the "fresh" broth. Pasteur then demonstrated his real genius. He now proceeded to feed the chickens that had recovered the bacilli in the fresh culture. They no longer became sick; they had become immune. Then, as with the wine experiment, he performed a controlled experiment, not only once but many times, which proved conclusively that chickens could be immunized against cholera.

His next problem—again one that posed an economic threat—had to do with anthrax, a disease that was spreading epidemically among the sheep of France. Applying what he had learned in his chicken studies, his results were spectacular and epoch-making. On May 5, 1881, he performed his famous experiment with two groups of sheep. He injected one group of twenty-five sheep with anthrax vaccine and in no way treated another group of the same number. By June 2 of that year, all the untreated sheep were dead and all the treated sheep were alive.

Pasteur then turned to rabies in human beings, at that time one of man's most feared diseases, since it invariably proved fatal. Applying what he had learned about disease in wine, silkworms, chickens, and sheep, he developed a vaccine to prevent rabies. In this way Pasteur became the father of preventive medicine by discovering the principle of vaccination.

If at this juncture the class has mastered the principles of thesis-sentence organization, the teacher may want to assign chapters in the second half of this book, especially those chapters entitled "*Fact* Statements" and "*Opinion* Statements," in order that the class may become aware of the nature of *evidence*, which is essential to the proper development of paragraphs.

Suggested HOW Topics

1. How the Atlantic cable was laid
2. How the human heart works
3. How the Catholic mass is performed
4. How Troy was rediscovered
5. How Eli Whitney invented the cotton gin
6. How an electron tube works
7. How Americans built the Panama Canal
8. One way of making a Japanese rock garden
9. How one species of plant was improved
10. How our nerves work
11. How Crete was rediscovered
12. How our solar system was formed
13. How a certain fossil was formed
14. How a transistor (generator, airplane, submarine, atomic reactor, etc.) works
15. How the steam engine was invented
16. How the pyramids were erected
17. How Alexander Hamilton was killed
18. How Leon Trotsky was ousted
19. How the Russians conducted the Battle of Berlin
20. How the Allies seized Casablanca during World War II
21. How the Constitutional Convention was conducted
22. How Leo Tolstoy became a mystic
23. How passive resistance was used by Mahatma Gandhi
24. How a diesel engine works
25. How tobacco is cured
26. How whiskey is distilled
27. How cigarettes are manufactured
28. How to play a certain game
29. How bronze casting is done
30. How to administer first aid to a heart-attack victim
31. How black-and-white film is developed
32. How a particular chemical experiment is performed
33. How X-rays are taken
34. How rubber (maple syrup) is extracted from trees
35. How a piano produces sound
36. How a famous crime was solved
37. How methane is produced
38. How a computer program is written
39. How sky-diving is performed
40. How the human digestive system works

Contrast Topics

Contrast is designed to show nontrivial *differences* between two or more sets. (*Comparison* is designed to show nontrivial *similarities* between two or more sets.) Topics that call for (1) contrast, (2) comparison, or (3) both contrast and comparison of ideas, objects, characters, terms, or attitudes are only sophisticated versions of *what* or *why* topics, depending upon whether they call for information or for opinion plus information. For instance, the first topic below ("The Ford and Carter administrations") can be treated as a *what* contrast topic if we simply report the key differences between the two administrations. It can also be treated as a *why* contrast topic if, in addition, we argue why one administration is superior to the other.

This topic can also be treated in terms of *comparison*. For instance, we can report the essential similarities between the two administrations. However, in order to explain the methodology of *contrast* themes, we shall arbitrarily consider the topics below to be exclusively of a contrast nature.

| **Examples A:** **CONTRAST Topics** | 1. The Ford and Carter administrations |

Examples A:
CONTRAST Topics

1. The Ford and Carter administrations
2. TV good guys and bad guys
3. Thomas Jefferson and Alexander Hamilton
4. The American pioneers and Americans today
5. Theories of free will and of determinism
6. Liberal arts courses and technical training courses
7. Rembrandt and Picasso
8. Beethoven and Mozart
9. The literary techniques of Ernest Hemingway and William Faulkner

Contrast topics, like *what* and *why* topics, can be organized by some form of the thesis sentence, though sometimes only one element may be specified if it is crucial. See *Examples B* below.

Examples B:
Thesis Sentences for
CONTRAST Topics

1. TV good guys differ from TV bad guys in being handsomer, stronger, and quicker on the draw.
   Using the symbol S_1 to designate the first set (TV good guys) and the symbol S_2 to designate the second set (TV bad guys), we can reduce this form of the thesis sentence to the following formulation: **S_1 and S_2 differ in respect to three elements** (handsomer, stronger, quicker on the draw).
2. Thomas Jefferson and Alexander Hamilton differed in their attitudes toward

the common man and hence in their ideas concerning the need for a strong central government. **S_1 and S_2 differ in respect to two elements.**

3. American pioneers and Americans today differ in their sense of self-worth. **S_1 and S_2 differ in respect to one element.**

Exercises A

1. What is meant by S_1? By S_2?
2. If we were to write elaborate essays, might we also have an S_3 and S_4 in our thesis sentence?
3. Choose three *contrast* topics (suggested topics appear at the end of this chapter) and construct a thesis sentence for each of them. Title your paper: Three Thesis Sentences Designed for Three *Contrast* Topics. **Be sure to avoid triviality**. If you treat a subject as a *why* topic, be sure your thesis is controversial. If you treat a subject as a *what* topic, be sure your thesis *or* its elements *or* both are not self-evident. For example, the points of contrast in the thesis sentence "Thomas Jefferson and Alexander Hamilton differed in age, height, and color of hair" are self-evident and therefore trivial. Moreover, the two sets need a point or points crucial to both of them if the contrast is not to be absurdly trivial. The thesis sentence "Thomas Jefferson differs from an imbecile in respect to intellectual and social habits" is ludicrously trivial.
4. Explain which one of the three thesis sentences in *Examples B* above seems most trivial. Which least? (Ignore the possibility that a first-class writer might produce more interesting results with a trivial-seeming topic than a third-class writer with a significant-seeming topic.)

As has been indicated, *contrast* topics can be organized by means of the thesis sentence. The method of organization is explained below.

Example C: Organization of Simple CONTRAST Topics

First paragraph.
A thesis sentence asserting that S_1 and S_2 can be contrasted in respect to one element. (For example: American pioneers and Americans today differ in their sense of self-worth.)

Second paragraph.
S_1 considered in respect to the one element. (In this paragraph no attempt need be made to contrast S_1 with S_2. The chief concern here is to present the information that will become the basis for contrast in paragraph 3. Thus, we would limit our discussion in this paragraph to the sense of self-worth that American pioneers felt.)

Third paragraph.
S_2 considered in respect to the one element (how modern Americans have lost their sense of self-worth) and how the element of this set differs from the element of S_1 (the self-worth that American pioneers felt). The student theme that appears below should make this analysis clear.

Exercises B

Analyze the theme below by answering these questions.

1. Identify S_1, S_2, and the element in the thesis sentence.
2. What is the crux of the second paragraph? Does it fulfill part of the proposal

of the thesis sentence? If so, identify by symbols that part which it does explain.

3. What is the crux of the third paragraph? Does it fulfill the rest of the proposal of the thesis sentence? If so, identify by symbols that part which it explains.

4. Quite specific points of contrast are made in the third paragraph. Cite instances of such contrasts.

5. Is the subject treated as a *what* or *why* topic? Explain.

A CONTRAST Theme Having Two Sets and One Element

AMERICAN PIONEERS AND AMERICANS TODAY*

American pioneers and Americans today differ in their sense of self-worth.

Because they had confidence in themselves and self-respect, pioneers had the courage to take risks and the hardihood to struggle for what they wanted. Unhappy with the Eastern towns, with the lack of opportunity for adventure or freedom, they fitted out their wagons and began the months-long trek to the prairies of the Dakotas or the wilderness of the Oregon Territory. Though always without luxuries and often falling short of necessities, they kept pushing their cattle-drawn caravans farther and farther westward. Finally, hundreds of miles from civilization—from doctors, general stores, schools, churches, and often miles from their nearest neighbors—they staked out their claims, built their sod huts or log cabins, and began clearing and breaking ground, though the method they used was as laborious as in the time of the Pharaohs—a hand-plow pulled by cattle. Some of these pioneers went hungry before the first harvest; many of them had to fight off squatters contending for their land or Indians who had taken to the warpath; and all of them had to endure the privations of the wilderness—loneliness, sickness, sometimes the death of loved ones. But, as Paine once wrote, "it is dearness only that gives every thing its value." Thus, through it all, they had the sense of freedom, of fulfillment, of shaping their own destinies, a sense that can come only from a direct confrontation with the realities of life, however harsh they may be.

Typical modern Americans, however, seem to have lost their confidence and feel a sense of unworthiness. They run few risks, and those who yearn for a sense of life seldom have the hardihood to make a break from their settled ways. Instead, they fall into the patterns of the sociologists' casebooks. They become the "other-directed" ones, or the "organization men," or the "status seekers." The trains and automobiles taking them from their suburbs to the city have to substitute for the westward trek in the Conestoga wagons. The paper work and conferences at the office, or their spectator sports, have to serve for the life-and-death encounters with the squatters or Indians. The sense of desperation that arises from this erosion of self-confidence, of vitality and meaning, is so widespread that it may even account for the popularity of TV westerns. These programs seem to present to such people at least an image

*This student theme was "inspired" by a reading of Ole Rölvaag's *Giants in the Earth*; John Steinbeck's "A Leader of the People"; and a number of encyclopedia articles on pioneers.

of the kind of freedom and self-fulfillment they desire but that, because of insecurity, they have to experience vicariously. It is out of this insecurity that most Americans nowadays hedge themselves with savings accounts, insurance policies, and retirement plans. Death may release them from their misery, but surely not old age and retirement. If now they suffer from that modern disease called "week-end neurosis" when on holidays they are left to their own devices and are confronted by their naked consciences, what will it be like when they have one prolonged holiday to contemplate the waste they have made of their lives? What at that time will substitute for the sense of self-worth that the pioneers had and could rightfully feel in reflecting upon their lives?

For longer and more involved themes, the procedure we have discussed in *Example C* is simply extended to include more sets, *or* more points of contrast, *or* both. If you increase the number of sets to be discussed, you must also increase the number of your paragraphs proportionately. See *Example D* below.

**Example D:
Organization of
CONTRAST Topics
Having Three Sets and
One Element**

First paragraph.
A thesis sentence asserting that S_1, S_2, and S_3 can be contrasted in respect to one element. (For instance: Samuel Seabury, John Dickinson, and Thomas Paine differed in their views toward the impending Revolutionary War.)

Second paragraph.
S_1 considered in respect to the element. (For instance: Samuel Seabury was a Tory who much preferred the peaceful and legal rule of King George III to the violent and illegal domination of King Mob, and who therefore opposed the revolution.)

Third paragraph.
S_2 considered in respect to the element and how the element of this set contrasts with the element of S_1. (For instance: John Dickinson was a Moderate who, though he felt that England had imposed some tyrannical measures such as the Stamp Tax upon the colonials, preferred to exhaust all peaceful and legal means of achieving revocation of those measures and reconciliation with England before resorting to the upheaval of a revolution. He differed from Seabury, who felt that England was acting entirely within her legal rights and that it was the colonists who were acting illegally by convoking the Continental Congress, by boycotting British goods, and by searching colonial houses to see who had violated the boycott.)

Fourth paragraph.
S_3 considered in respect to the element and how the element of this set contrasts with the element of S_1 and S_2. (For instance: Thomas Paine was a Radical who wanted not only revolution as a means of forcing England to make concessions to the colonies, but urged the colonials to wage a war for total independence from England. He differed from Seabury, who felt that the colonies were at fault, not England, and from Dickinson, who preferred reconciliation to violence and, at worst, revolution to independence.)

If, instead of increasing the number of sets, you wish to increase only the number of elements to be discussed, the organization remains fundamentally as we have described it. The only thing affected is the number of ideas you have to play with within each paragraph. The student theme below illustrates this variation in number of elements; *Example E* analyzes the methodology.

Example E: Organization of CONTRAST Topics Having Two Sets and Two Elements

First paragraph.
A thesis sentence asserting that S_1 and S_2 can be contrasted in respect to two elements (*a* and *b*).

Second paragraph.
S_1 considered in respect to the two elements. (Since the two elements are elements of S_1, they are, or ought to be, related and can be treated together. In this paragraph no attempt need be made to contrast S_1 and S_2. The chief concern here is to present the evidence that will become the basis for contrast in paragraph 3.)

Third paragraph.
S_2 considered in respect to the two elements and how the two elements of this set contrast with the two elements of S_1.

Exercises C

Analyze the theme below by answering these questions.

1. Identify S_1 and S_2 and the elements (*a* and *b*) in the thesis sentence.
2. In the second paragraph are the elements related? Explain.
3. In the third paragraph is S_2 considered in respect to the two elements? Explain.
4. In the third paragraph do the two elements of S_2 contrast with the two elements of S_1? Identify statements in the paragraph that make this contrast pointed.
5. Is the subject treated as a *what* or *why* topic? Explain.

A CONTRAST Theme Having Two Sets and Two Elements

THOMAS JEFFERSON AND ALEXANDER HAMILTON CONTRASTED*

Thomas Jefferson and Alexander Hamilton differed in their attitudes toward the common man and hence in their ideas concerning the need for a strong central government.

Jefferson had the belief that the common man was perfectible, a fact that accounts for his great faith in democracy. To enable the common man to perfect himself, he believed in universal education, in free intellectual inquiry, and in the exercise of the greatest individual freedom compatible with the liberties of others. A strong federal government, he felt, was bound to work at cross purposes with a democracy whose major purpose, as he conceived it, was to encourage the moral, physical, and intellectual perfection of its citizens. He feared that, unless the powers of a federal government were

*This student theme is based upon James Truslow Adams, *Our Business Civilization: Some Aspects of American Culture* (New York: Albert and Charles Boni, 1929); Vernon Louis Parrington, *Main Currents in American Thought* (New York: Harcourt, Brace and Co., 1930), 1: 292–307; and Claude G. Bowers, *Jefferson and Hamilton: The Struggle for Democracy in America* (Boston: Houghton Mifflin Co., 1925).

severely limited, federal power would fall into the hands of an oligarchy of wealth that would impose its own will upon the majority, curtail their liberties, enslave their minds, and thus subvert the purposes of a democracy. To offset this possibility, Jefferson wanted to extend the right to vote to every man, a privilege not nearly so universally available then as now. For this reason too he wanted to limit the powers of a federal government largely to the right to negotiate with foreign nations and to deal with continental problems that no one state could handle independently.

Alexander Hamilton, however, believed that the common man was evil by nature, not good, as Jefferson thought. "The People," he said, "is a great Beast," given to passion, not reason, to selfishness, not altruism. To him, the idea that the common man was perfectible was simply the delusion of a visionary. Hence, he believed that for the public good, as well as to protect the common man from his own mischief, a strong central government was not only highly desirable but absolutely necessary. Thus, unlike Jefferson, who wanted the least government possible, Hamilton wanted the most powerful government possible. Thus, instead of urging universal education and universal manhood suffrage as Jefferson had, Hamilton was indifferent, if not opposed, to both. Human nature, he felt, could not be changed by education, except to make it craftier in achieving its own selfish ends. And to give the masses the vote was, as he saw it, a dangerous thing indeed, for it would put power into the hands of the riffraff.

How To Contrast Two Sets Simultaneously

A more sophisticated but no more difficult way of organizing a *contrast* theme is to deal with two sets simultaneously and with the elements of the sets alternately. The methods for organizing "regular" and "sophisticated" *contrast* themes are shown below.

Regular CONTRAST Organization	Sophisticated CONTRAST Organization
First Paragraph	
Thesis sentence asserting that S_1 and S_2 can be contrasted in respect to two elements.	Thesis sentence asserting that S_1 and S_2 can be contrasted in respect to two elements.
Second Paragraph	
S_1 considered in respect to the two elements.	S_1 and S_2 considered in respect to the first element.
Third Paragraph	
S_2 considered in respect to the two elements.	S_1 and S_2 considered in respect to the second element.

Whether to adopt *regular contrast organization* or *sophisticated contrast organization* depends in great part upon one key factor: how familiar you can expect your reader to be with the sets and their elements. In *sophisticated* themes, essays, and articles, the writer typically addresses a specialized audience who are concerned only with the writer's special contribution to a subject with which they are very familiar. For example, if a research doctor wants to publish an article in the *Journal of the American Medical Association* on a new technique he has developed for performing open-heart surgery and, in the process, show that his technique has virtues that present techniques lack, he would hardly explain the physiology of the heart or the instruments used in open-heart surgery. He would know that his audience would be concerned only with an explanation of his new surgical technique and the evidence for its superiority over present ones. If, however, his is a lay audience, the result may be only bewilderment.

The theme that appears below illustrates *sophisticated contrast organization* based on the analysis that appears above.

Exercises D   Analyze the theme below by answering these questions.

1. What are the sets being contrasted? What elements are being contrasted?
2. Identify the main points of contrast discussed in the theme itself.
3. Do you find the organization of this theme easier or more difficult to follow than the organization found in the previous specimens of *contrast* themes?
4. Is this theme directed to the general reader or to a specialized reader?
5. Is the subject treated as a *what* or *why* topic? Is the author, in other words, concerned with presenting information, or is he concerned with presenting an opinion plus information?

A Theme Illustrating Sophisticated CONTRAST Organization

EURIPIDES' AND ROBINSON JEFFERS' *MEDEA**

A study of the Euripides and Jeffers versions of *Medea* shows that Jeffers improved the original significantly by reshaping the leading characters and by making the play more dramatic.

Jeffers' chief improvement lies in his characterization of Medea herself. She emerges in this play as a more complex and more intensely human protagonist than in the original. She is not so much the vicious woman whose crimes are all conceived well in advance as a woman who, however impelled to vengeance, continually wavers in her decisions. This vacillation makes her crimes ones of passion rather than of calculation and serves to evoke a greater pity for her. Moreover, Medea shows a far greater love for her children in Jeffers' version, which makes her final act of double infanticide all the more terrible. Lastly, she becomes the typical Jeffers heroine in search of "wholeness," an urge that gives her acts a rationale other than that of mere desire for revenge. Jeffers also improves upon Euripides by gaining sympathy for all the other leading characters as well, an achievement especially noteworthy in the case of Jason. In Euripides, sympathy is almost wholly lacking for him, but Jeffers, by having Jason show a more intense love for his children, gives him a redeeming quality that wins our pity. Euripides also shows Creon's daughter as suffering from pride and, by implication, as deserving of her fearful death, but Jeffers makes her an innocent victim, which again elicits our pity.

*This essay was written by one of the authors to exemplify *sophisticated contrast organization*.

Technically, Jeffers heightens the drama of the play too. In Euripides' *Medea*, for example, Aegeus is brought on stage quite mechanically so that Medea can ask him for refuge after she has committed the atrocities she is planning. In Jeffers' *Medea*, Aegeus is sought out by the Nurse and comes to Medea only under persuasion, by which technique the mechanicalness of his entrance is eliminated and the Nurse, incidentally, is further integrated into the play. Moreover, in keeping with Euripides' characterization of Medea, Medea implores Aegeus for refuge, knowing in advance what crimes she will commit and what consequences she will have to escape. In Jeffers' characterization, Medea ignores Aegeus at first. When she notices him, it is only to recite her tale of wrongs, even as she recited them to the Corinthian women. It is only at the Nurse's prompting that she pridefully and even spitefully asks Aegeus for sanctuary, though she does not yet know what form her vengeance will take. What is without doubt the greatest dramatic element in this scene, an element that is entirely lacking in the original, is that Aegeus himself is the one who suggests to Medea the crowning horror of her revenge. In asking Medea to unriddle the oracle's utterance so that he can become potent, Aegeus says: "When death comes, Medea, / It is, for a childless man, utter despair, darkness, extinction. / One's children / Are the life after death." It is only then that Medea, who has been brooding upon an apt form of revenge, seizes upon the idea of infanticide: "Do you feel it so? / Then—if you had a dog-eyed enemy and needed absolute vengeance—you'd kill / The man's children first. Unchild him, ha? / And then unlife him." The chorus too, as Jeffers handles it, becomes a well-integrated element of the play instead of merely occupying the conventional and secondary role that it does in Euripides. Jeffers accomplishes this by having all the leading characters speak to the chorus at one time or another, whereas Euripides allows Creon, Aegeus, and Jason to ignore the chorus entirely. Furthermore, "set speeches" that are nondramatic because of their length and narrative quality are broken up or replaced by the give-and-take of dialogue. An excellent example of this is provided by the messenger's speech. In Euripides' version the messenger's account of the death of Creon and his daughter is the longest speech in the play and is pure narrative. Jeffers, to eliminate this nondramatic feature, introduces a second messenger who, together with the Nurse, piles horror on horror; and even these speeches are continually interrupted by Medea, who pumps them for more of the gory details so that she may all the better satisfy her vindictiveness. Greek tragedy typically lets the outcome be known beforehand. Thus, in Euripides' play, Medea predicts exactly what will happen when she sends Jason and the children to Creon's daughter with gifts. The account of the messenger, therefore, simply confirms what the audience has been led to expect and the effect of shock and terror is thereby minimized. Jeffers, by deemphasizing this feature of prediction, makes pity and terror all the greater.

In these ways Jeffers has performed the monumental feat of adapting a Greek tragedy to modern tastes without doing violence to the diction, the drama, and the power which we associate with the original. If anything, he has improved the poetic qualities of the play, as he did the characterization and dramatic qualities of the play. His feat, in the revival of Greek drama, stands as a triumphant example of literary adaptation.

The paragraphs in this essay are obviously too long. This condition can be easily corrected by dividing the elements and reparagraphing the essay accordingly. The first element is "reshaping the leading characters." This element divides into two—namely, (1) the protagonist Medea and (2) other leading characters (a division which would make two paragraphs instead of one). Likewise, the second element "making the play more dramatic" divides into four according to what is affected by Jeffers' integrative techniques—namely, (1) leading characters, (2) chorus, (3) set speeches, and (4) Medea's prediction (a division which would make four paragraphs). Thus, the entire essay, reparagraphed, would have eight paragraphs: the six specified, the paragraph containing the thesis sentence, and the paragraph containing the conclusion.

CONTRAST by negation

Another way of organizing a contrast theme is *contrast by negation*. By stating, in effect, that S_1 does not possess the elements of S_2, a writer automatically contrasts two sets. This form of organization has only limited applicability since it can deal only with sets that are radically unlike in respect to many of their elements. A theme using this form of organization need have only two paragraphs, one consisting of a thesis sentence and the other consisting of a series of assertions. This form is exemplified by the selection below.

Exercises E

Analyze the selection below by answering these questions.

1. What two sets are being contrasted?
2. Identify each point of contrast as it appears in the selection.
3. Is the subject treated as a *what* or *why* topic? Explain.

A Selection Illustrating CONTRAST by negation

. . . It takes a great deal of [civilization] . . . to produce a little literature.

[For example,] . . . the negative side of the spectacle on which Hawthorne looked out, in his contemplative saunterings and reveries, might, indeed, with a little ingenuity, be made almost ludicrous; one might enumerate the items of high civilization, as it exists in other countries, which are absent from the texture of American life [contemporaneous with Hawthorne's] until it should become a wonder to know what was left. No State, in the European sense of the word, and indeed barely a specific national name. No sovereign, no court, no personal loyalty, no aristocracy, no church, no clergy, no army, no diplomatic service, no country gentlemen, no palaces, no castles, nor manors, nor old country houses, nor parsonages, nor thatched cottages, nor ivied ruins; no cathedrals, nor abbeys, nor little Norman churches; no great universities nor public schools—no Oxford, nor Eton, nor Harrow; no literature, no novels, no museums, no pictures, no political society, no sporting class—no

Epsom nor Ascot! Some such list as that might be drawn up of the absent things in American life—especially in the American life of forty years ago, the effect of which, upon an English or a French imagination, would probably as a general thing be appalling. The natural remark, in the almost lurid light of such an indictment, would be that if these things are left out, everything is left out.—From *Hawthorne* by Henry James.

CONTRAST as an Incidental Technique

Thus far we have explained how *contrast* topics can be organized. Contrast, however, can be used as an incidental technique within the body of themes. In such instances we usually find an item-by-item contrast within a single sentence and sometimes within whole paragraphs.

Below appear two literary examples of item-by-item contrast.

Selections Illustrating CONTRAST as Incidental Technique

The passage here uses this formula for contrast within each sentence: "If not *1*, then *2*. If not *3*, then *4*. If not *5*, then *6*."

If they [the Puritans] were unacquainted with the works of philosophers and poets, they were deeply read in the oracles of God. If their names were not found in the registers of heralds, they felt assured that they were recorded in the Book of Life. If their steps were not accompanied by a splendid train of menials, legions of ministering angels had charge over them.—From "Milton" by Thomas Babington Macaulay.

The passage here, though somewhat varied, may be explained by this formula: "God could have done *1* but did *2*; could have done *3* but did *4*; could have done *5* but did *6*."

"Strange, indeed, that you should not have suspected that your universe and its contents were only dreams, visions, fiction!* Strange, because they are so frankly and hysterically insane—like all dreams: a God who could make good children as easily as bad, yet preferred to make bad ones; who could have made every one of them happy, yet never made a single happy one; who made them prize their bitter life, yet stingily cut it short; who gave his angels eternal happiness unearned, yet required his other children to earn it; who gave his angels painless lives, yet cursed his other children with biting miseries and maladies of mind and body; who mouths justice and invented hell—mouths mercy and invented hell—mouths Golden Rules, and forgiveness multiplied by seventy times seven, and invented hell; who mouths morals to other people and has none himself; who frowns upon crimes, yet commits them all; who created man without invitation, then tries to shuffle the responsibility for man's acts upon man, instead of honorably placing it where it belongs, upon himself; and finally, with altogether divine obtuseness, invites this poor, abused slave to worship him! . . .

"You perceive, *now*, that these things are all impossible except in a dream. You perceive that they are pure and puerile insanities, the silly creations of an

* In this passage from Mark Twain's *The Mysterious Stranger*, a nephew of Satan is explaining to a boy in a medieval Austrian village that life is only a dream. We have included in this passage the "thesis" and the "conclusion"; the body of the passage, of course, consists of contrasting elements.

imagination that is not conscious of its freaks—in a word, that they are a dream, and you the maker of it. The dream-marks are all present; you should have recognized them earlier."

Exercise F

Construct a thesis sentence for a *contrast* topic that takes the form "S_1 differs from S_2 nontrivially in respect to one element" and develop a theme from that thesis sentence.

Suggested CONTRAST Topics

1. Two labor unions
2. Two comic strips
3. Training and vocational education
4. Two TV shows
5. The big city and the small town
6. Two recent movies (or plays)
7. Northerners and Southerners (Easterners and Westerners)
8. Two minority groups
9. Epicureanism and Stoicism
10. Large universities and small colleges
11. Public and private colleges
12. The French and American revolutions
13. Caesar and Brutus in Shakespeare's *Julius Caesar*
14. Protestants and Catholics
15. The Ptolemaic and Copernican systems
16. Alchemy and chemistry
17. The Salk and Sabin vaccines
18. The Julian and Gregorian Calendars
19. Astrology and astronomy
20. Two kinds of advertising (propaganda, child-rearing)
21. Two magazines
22. License and liberty
23. Two humorists
24. Two actors
25. Two playwrights
26. Two authors (Emerson and Thoreau; Wordsworth and Coleridge; Poe and Hawthorne)
27. Preferred and common stock
28. Two humanitarians
29. Private and public rights
30. Two kinds of courts
31. Two kinds of farming
32. Physical and psychological fatigue
33. Two kinds of mental disorders
34. Instinct and thought
35. Liquor and marijuana
36. Indoor and outdoor gardening

37. Two kinds of prisons
38. Two kinds of engines
39. An idealist and a realist
40. Two economic (political, social) ideas
41. External and internal reinforcement
42. Two psychologists (Carl Rogers and B. F. Skinner; Sigmund Freud and Carl Jung)
43. Free will and determinism
44. Rural and urban blight
45. Two breeds of dogs (cows, horses, etc.)
46. Two governors (representatives, teachers, etc.)
47. Indentured servitude and slavery
48. Mores and morality
49. Hoarders and spendthrifts
50. Two soap operas

5

Comparison Topics

Almost everything we said about *contrast* topics applies to *comparison* topics. *Comparison* topics, like *contrast* topics, are only sophisticated versions of *what* or *why* topics, depending upon whether they call for information or for opinion plus information. For instance, the first topic in *Examples A* below ("Compare urban and rural blight") can be treated as a *what* comparison topic if we simply report the similarities of blight in city and town. It can also be treated as a *why* comparison topic if, in addition, we argue that one kind of blight is less objectionable than the other.

These topics can also be treated in terms of *contrast*. For instance, we can obviously *contrast* city blight and town blight. However, in order to explain the methodology of *comparison* themes, we shall arbitrarily consider the topics below to be exclusively of a comparison nature.

Examples A:
COMPARISON Topics

Which of these topics would you prefer to consider as *what* comparison topics? As *why* comparison topics?

1. Compare urban and rural blight
2. Compare Mark Twain's *The Mysterious Stranger* and the fourth part of Jonathan Swift's *Gulliver's Travels*
3. Compare Abraham Lincoln and John F. Kennedy
4. Compare plants and human beings
5. Compare two soap operas
6. Compare two actors
7. Compare two breeds of dogs
8. Compare two minority groups
9. Compare two religions

Comparison topics can also be organized by means of the thesis sentence. See *Examples B* below.

Examples B:
Thesis Sentences for
COMPARISON Topics

1. Twain's *Mysterious Stranger* and the fourth part of Swift's *Gulliver's Travels* are alike in that both authors use animals as their norms and see the human race as degenerate.
   (Reduced to formula, this sentence reads: S_1 and S_2 are alike in respect to two elements.)
2. Abraham Lincoln and John F. Kennedy were alike in that both were witty,

Center for Teaching
The Westminster Schools

both were concerned about racial problems, and both were disliked by most Southerners.

(S_1 and S_2 are alike in respect to three elements.)

3. Plants and human beings seem strikingly alike in their biological adjustment to environment.

(S_1 and S_2 are alike in respect to one element.)

Exercise A

Choose three *comparison* topics and construct a thesis sentence for each of them. Title your paper: Three Thesis Sentences Designed for Three *Comparison* Topics. **Be sure to avoid triviality.** For the definition of triviality, see page 38 (*Exercises A*, Question 3).

In addition to the similarities already pointed out, *comparison* topics and *contrast* topics are alike in that they stimulate us to discover significant likenesses or significant differences between two or more sets and that they can be organized in precisely the same way (see the selection below).

Exercises B

Analyze the selection that appears below by answering these questions.

1. What two sets are being compared? For what purpose?
2. What is the topic sentence of paragraph two? Of paragraph three?
3. What conclusion does the writer reach? Is it trivial or nontrivial? Explain.
4. Does the writer treat his subject as a *what* or *why* topic? Explain.
5. By using our system of symbolic notation, analyze the organization of this selection.

A COMPARISON Essay Having Two Sets and One Element

PLANTS AND HUMAN BEINGS*

[Plants and human beings seem strikingly alike in their biological adjustment to environment.]

. . . The growth and movements of plants are characteristics based upon hereditary nature, and this includes the plant's ways of selecting and responding to environmental stimuli. No plant is infinitely adaptable. If its inherited characteristics of form and performance are very much out of harmony with its environment, or if it comes into competition with other plants better fitted to that environment, it does not flourish; it deals with its environment in its own variable but limited way, adapting to certain changes (perhaps even "learning") and resisting others, and if it fails to meet the conditions imposed, it perishes. The individual members of a species act somewhat alike, to the extent that environmental conditions can be found which no member of that species can endure, although the members of some other species may welcome them; but within the species' limits there is always, of course, individual variety permitting some to survive while others of the same species droop and die.

Biologically speaking, the rules seem to be very much the same for the hu-

*From *The Personal World: An Introduction to the Study of Personality* by Harold Grier McCurdy.

man species. Neither any single human being nor the species entire is infinitely adaptable. Limits are set upon us genetically. For example, it is probable that some human individuals respond very poorly to a bringing-up which most other members of the species would be able to tolerate or even enjoy. This is all that one need imply when stressing the importance of heredity. . . . There is the possibility that various kinds of personal qualities and patterns of behavior characterizing the individual are primarily rooted in the genes.

We said that the *purpose* of *contrast* themes was to discover meaningful differences between sets. In other words, we contrast sets not merely for compositional exercise but for intellectual ends: (1) to inform our reader or (2) to inform our reader and to present our opinion. For example, one of the *contrast* themes we have looked at ("Thomas Jefferson and Alexander Hamilton Contrasted," pages 41–42) was simply designed to inform the reader about certain crucial differences between the two men and to let him draw his own conclusions. Two other themes ("American Pioneers and Americans Today," pages 39–40, and "Euripides' and Robinson Jeffers' *Medea*," pages 43–44) were concerned with informing the reader *and* with presenting an opinion. Similarly, the *comparison* "theme" we have just looked at ("Plants and Human Beings") was designed to inform the reader and to suggest a point of view— namely, that conditions good for some plants and human beings may be bad for other plants and human beings, a view that constitutes a powerful biological argument against the enforcement of uniformity.

However, "Plants and Human Beings" represents a variation in that it is not comparison per se but *comparison by analogy*. **Analogy is the process by which we compare one thing to another in order to determine whether certain similarities suggest other probable similarities.** For instance, when scientists presume that what happens to experimental animals in cancer research can happen to human beings if similar experiments were done upon them, they are making a *comparison by analogy*. Thus, aside from the kind of *comparison* theme we have been discussing (e.g., "Homer's *Odyssey* and James Joyce's *Ulysses* are alike in that they use the same general myth"), there are other kinds that are analogical in character, as illustrated below.

The Purposes of COMPARISON BY ANALOGY

Comparison by analogy serves a large variety of purposes: (1) for argumentation, (2) for theorizing, (3) for explanation (such as making an abstraction concrete, an abstruse concept simple, or the unfamiliar familiar), and (4) for inspiration. The selections below illustrate these various purposes.

ANALOGY for ARGUMENTATIVE Purposes

That man has no free will but only the illusion of free will is made evident by the following analogy. Suppose we hurl a rock in the air and, in mid-career, it is suddenly endowed with self-consciousness. Would not the rock think it was moving of its own free will? Surely, we are like the rock that without free will was hurled into space. We too have been endowed with self-consciousness. And we too have the illusion that we are moving of our own free will.— Adapted from Spinoza's *Ethics*.

Exercises C

1. In the above paragraph, what two sets are being compared? In respect to which major element are they being compared?
2. If we grant the legitimacy of the comparison, must we also grant the conclusion? Explain.
3. On what grounds might we reject the legitimacy of this comparison?

Analogy for THEORIZING Purposes

This paragraph *compares* Venus with Earth. Venus, to one degree or another, satisfies all conditions for life except that of temperature. Thus, indications are that there is no life on this planet.

This paragraph *compares* Mars with Earth. It is found that Mars has, to one degree or another, water, an atmosphere, temperatures conceivably suitable for life, some oxygen, and possibly carbon dioxide (if its surface, which appears "greener in summer," is evidence of vegetation). Thus Mars seems to satisfy the five conditions necessary for life.

This leaves for consideration only Venus and Mars.* Venus is the least satisfactory planet to observe. She is surrounded by an atmosphere so hazy that it hides her solid surface. There is a large quantity of carbon dioxide in her atmosphere, but too little oxygen or water vapor to measure. The maximum surface temperature is probably about that of boiling water. This indicates strongly that there is no life on Venus. It is, however, very interesting to note that, except for the higher temperatures, conditions on Venus are decidedly similar to the theoretical picture of what our Earth was like before life started on it.

Turning finally to the one remaining possibility, we find that Mars has a thin atmosphere, so that we can see the surface clearly. The planet has seasons like our own, and the heat-measures indicate that, in the tropics, the temperature rises above freezing (to about 50 degrees) every day and falls below freezing every night. At the poles, the maximum temperature in summer is also about 50 degrees; the winters must be very cold. White caps form at the poles of Mars every winter, and shrink almost to nothing in summer. This immediately suggests snow, and the temperatures confirm this beyond reasonable doubt. Hence there is water on Mars. The polar snows are, however, probably only a few inches thick, for spectroscopic observations show that there is little water vapor in the atmosphere. They indicate, too, that there is at present very little oxygen on Mars—not over a thousandth part of the amount above an equal area on Earth. But there is strong reason to believe that there once was oxygen there, for most of the surface has the characteristic yellow-red color of weathered, oxidized material. There is nothing like this color on any other of the planets. The moon, for example, which has no atmosphere, does not have a single red or yellow patch on it. Mars, then, matches closely the theoretical picture of a planet in a late stage, when rock weathering has used up almost all the oxygen of the atmosphere. The darker parts of its surface show seasonal changes and are larger and greener in summer than in winter. They probably represent surviving vegetation; but it has not been proved that some other explanation may not be possible. Whether animal life ever existed on Mars and whether it has been able to survive is not known.

* The writer is theorizing by analogy that other planets cannot have life on them unless they have certain crucial factors in common with Earth. At this point he has eliminated all planets but two.

This paragraph theorizes about the probability of life on planets of other solar systems.

Outside the system composed of our sun and its circulating planets, there was no evidence for the existence of other planets till 1949. Since then, precise photographic observations show that several of the nearest stars have invisible companions revolving about them which can be detected because their attraction causes the bright stars to move in slightly wavy curves. The smallest of these companions are certainly dark bodies, and may fairly be called planets. We can find small companions of this sort only if they belong to some one of the few hundred stars which lie nearest to the sun. Among the many millions of more distant stars, there are very likely great numbers of them. Though the conditions for habitability are fairly stringent, there may well be thousands or more of habitable worlds among them.

This paragraph presents the theoretical conclusions drawn from the *comparisons* made.

Thus, in our own sun-planet system, there are only three possibly habitable bodies—Venus, the Earth, and Mars. Life is in full blast on the Earth, and has probably existed, and may still exist, on Mars. That is, life has scored twice out of three tries. It is therefore reasonable to suppose that, within the vast expanse of the universe, there may be very many other bodies which are actually the abodes of life. Of course, it is hardly reasonable to suppose that on all habitable worlds, life is in the same stage of evolution as on Earth today. On some there may be living creatures far surpassing mankind in intelligence and character.—Henry Norris Russell in *Serving through Science*.

ANALOGIES for EXPLANATORY Purposes

The chemical elements tend to be less familiar to most people than the alphabet. By making a *comparison* between letters and elements and between words and substances, one prepares the reader for a readier grasp of the subject.

The 26 letters of our alphabet make up all the thousands of words in our language. Similarly, the more than 100 elements make up all the thousands of substances in the universe. For this reason the elements are sometimes called the chemical alphabet.

The thesis sentence suggests that the rules of life-playing are *comparable* in difficulty and complication to the rules of chess-playing.

It is a very plain and elementary truth that the life, the fortune, and the happiness of every one of us, and more or less of those who are connected with us, . . . depend upon our knowing something of the rules of a game infinitely more difficult and complicated than chess.

This paragraph *compares* life to chess in a variety of ways.

It is a game which has been played for untold ages, every man and woman of us being one of the two players in a game of his or her own. The chessboard is the world, the pieces are the phenomena of the universe, the rules of the game are what we call the laws of Nature. The player on the other side is hidden from us. We know that his play is always fair, just and patient. But also we know, to our cost, that he never overlooks a mistake, or makes the smallest allowance for ignorance. To the man who plays well, the highest stakes are paid, with that sort of overflowing generosity with which the strong shows delight in strength. And one who plays ill is checkmated—without haste, but without remorse. My metaphor will remind some of you of the famous picture in which Retzsch has depicted Satan playing at chess with man for his soul. Substitute for the mocking fiend in that picture a calm, strong angel who is playing for love, as we say, and would rather lose than win—and I should accept it as an image of human life.

This paragraph draws the conclusion, partly by implication, that if all we have to learn is chess, then anything that pretends to teach us chess, but does not, cannot be called teaching. Similarly, education is that which teaches us the rules of life. Anything that does not teach us these rules cannot be called education.

Well, what I mean by Education is learning the rules of this mighty game. In other words, education is the instruction of the intellect in the laws of Nature, under which name I include not merely things and their forces, but men and their ways; and the fashioning of the affections and of the will into an earnest and loving desire to move in harmony with those laws. For me, education means neither more nor less than this. Anything which professes to call itself education must be tried by this standard, and if it fails to stand the test, I will not call it education, whatever may be the force of authority, or of numbers, upon the other side.—From Thomas Henry Huxley's "A Liberal Education and Where to Find It" in *Science and Education*.

Exercises D

1. Formulate a thesis sentence for the above essay so that it takes this form: S_1 and S_2 are alike in respect to one element.
2. Does the analogy used by Huxley help to clarify the abstract concept of education? If so, how?

Analogy for INSPIRATIONAL Purposes

Every one has heard the story which has gone the rounds of New England, of a strong and beautiful bug which came out of the dry leaf of an old table of apple-tree wood, which had stood in a farmer's kitchen for sixty years, first in Connecticut, and afterward in Massachusetts,—from an egg deposited in the living tree many years earlier still, as appeared by counting the annual layers beyond it; which was heard gnawing out for several weeks, hatched perchance by the heat of an urn. Who does not feel his faith in a resurrection and immortality strengthened by hearing of this? Who knows what beautiful and winged life, whose egg has been buried for ages under many concentric layers of woodenness in the dead dry life of society, deposited at first in the alburnum of the green and living tree, which has been gradually converted into the semblance of its well-seasoned tomb,—heard perchance gnawing out now for years by the astonished family of man, as they sat round the festive board,—may unexpectedly come forth from amidst society's most trivial and handselled furniture, to enjoy its perfect summer life at last!—From Thoreau's *Walden*.

Exercise E

In the excerpt from Thoreau's *Walden* above, what sets are being compared? In respect to what element? Why is Thoreau's purpose here considered inspirational?

It should be stressed that *comparisons by analogy*, however forcefully expressed, can only open up avenues of investigation; they cannot in themselves be offered as proof. A method of treating cancer in experimental animals, for instance, may suggest a treatment for cancer in human beings; but the most forceful exposition of this possibility cannot prove that the method will work for human beings. To determine whether the treatment will indeed prove effective depends not on forcefulness of expression but upon investigation— in this instance, by experimentation with human patients. To cite another case, George Lyman Kittredge, the famous Shakespearean scholar, wanted once and for all to explode the method of "proof by analogy" as applied to Shakespeare. For certain scholars of his time were arguing that Shakespeare's plays were to be read as "veiled allegories on contemporary personages and political events," and they were therefore searching the Bard's plays for analogical counterparts in Elizabethan London. Professor Kittredge, with tongue in cheek, proceeded to use exactly the same method by offering a point-by-point comparison of *Romeo and Juliet* and a contemporary scandal called the Thomas Overbury murder case. He concluded his quite persuasive comparison in this way:

I have said enough, I trust, to convince you that Shakespeare must have had this scandalous affair in mind when he wrote his tragedy of *Romeo and Juliet*.

Certainly my case is much stronger than that of any of my contemporaries in this kind of topical interpretation of Shakespeare.

There is, however, one slight obstacle: a difficulty about dates.

Shakespeare wrote *Romeo and Juliet* not later than 1595; it was printed in 1597, and again in 1599.

The first marriage of Lady Frances took place in 1606, the divorce and second marriage in 1613, the murder of Overbury in 1613, and the trials in 1615 and 1616.

Are you satisfied with my *reductio ad absurdum?*—From *New Light on Romeo and Juliet*.

COMPARISONS for Incidental Purposes

Comparisons can also be made *incidentally* within the body of themes for various purposes (not the least of which is vividness of expression) by devices belonging to the class of *figures of speech*. These devices are called *personification, simile, metaphor,* and *allusion*.

Figures of Speech Used for COMPARISON

Personification is the process by which an abstraction is rendered less abstract by comparing it to a generalized person in respect to one or more human elements.

1. Time is a great legalizer.—H. L. Mencken
2. Self-interest speaks all sorts of tongues, and plays all sorts of roles, even that of disinterestedness.—de La Rochefoucauld

3. Athens was the mother of the arts.—John Milton
4. Pale Death with impartial tread beats at the poor man's cottage door and at the palaces of kings.—Horace

Simile is the process by which two dissimilar things are compared in respect to one or more of their elements. *Simile* typically uses words such as *like* or *as*, but other connective words are possible.

1. Laws are like cobwebs, which may catch small flies, but let wasps and hornets break through.—Jonathan Swift
2. Though I speak with the tongues of men and of angels, and have not charity, I am become as sounding brass or a tinkling cymbal.—St. Paul
3. [Hawthorne] has a great deep intellect which drops down into the universe like a plummet.—Herman Melville
4. Man is like a reed, the weakest in nature, but he is a thinking reed.—Blaise Pascal.

Metaphor works exactly like simile, except that it has no "signs" such as *like* or *as*, for which reason *metaphor* is sometimes called *condensed simile*.

1. Everyone is a moon and has a dark side which he never shows to anybody.—Mark Twain
2. Eden is that old-fashioned House
   We dwell in every day.—Emily Dickinson
3. Fie, . . . brother bard; with good fruit of your own,
   Can't you let Neighbor Emerson's orchards alone?—James Russell Lowell
4. [We are] but . . . Pieces of the Game He plays
   Upon this Chequer-board of Nights and Days;
   　Hither and thither moves, and checks, and slays,
   And one by one back in the Closet lays.—Edward Fitzgerald

Allusion is the process by which two different things are compared by suggestion in respect to one or more elements. By the same logic *allusion* can be used for *contrast*. The first three examples below illustrate *allusion for comparison*; the fourth illustrates *allusion for contrast*.

Allusion for Comparison

1. The architect of my chimney must have had the pyramid of Cheops before him.—Herman Melville
2. For numbers and for carnage [this battle of the ants] was an Austerlitz or Dresden.—Henry David Thoreau
   (*Austerlitz* was the scene of Napoleon's victory in 1805 over the Austrian and Russian armies. *Dresden* was the place where Napoleon in 1813 won his last great battle.)
3. "A Daniel come to judgment!"—Shakespeare
   (Shylock makes this exclamation in the famous courtroom scene of *The Merchant of Venice* when Portia seems to be siding with him. The allusion is to the Daniel mentioned in the apocryphal Book of Susanna. He is the judge who delivers Susanna from her false accusers.)

Allusion for Contrast

4. Some mute inglorious Milton here may rest,
   Some Cromwell guiltless of his country's blood.—Thomas Gray
   (In contemplating a country churchyard, Gray thinks that opportunity for
   good and evil alike had never occurred to the people who lived in the village; hence, the allusions to John Milton and Oliver Cromwell. The allusions are related: Milton, the great poet, was the Latin secretary of Cromwell, who led the Puritan Revolution in England. The word *inglorious* is
   used by Gray to mean *ungloried*.)

Allusion by Paraphrase

Allusion by paraphrase is another form of allusion, and serves the purpose of
both comparison and contrast. If the allusion is not to be obscure, the paraphrase must echo a well-known expression. The first example below involves
a *comparison*; the second, a *contrast*.

1. A crowd flowed over London Bridge, so many,
   I had not thought death had undone so many.—T. S. Eliot
   (When, according to his *Inferno*, Dante enters Hell, he sees such a crowd of
   people that he thinks, "I would never have believed that death had undone
   so many." By this *allusion by paraphrase*, Eliot is able to suggest a comparison between modern London and Hell.)
2. Malt does more than Milton can
   To Justify God's ways to man.—A. E. Housman
   (In his invocation to *Paradise Lost*, Milton said his intention was to "justify
   the ways of God to man." In this *allusion by paraphrase* Housman is able
   to contrast his perception of God-man relations with Milton's intention by
   suggesting that God's ways are so unjustified that only malt [beer and ale]
   can enable men to bear "God's ways to man.")

These figures of speech can occur in any combination, so long as logic is
preserved. (Unless one *intends* humor, he should not write such Goldwynisms
as "They're always biting the hand that lays the golden eggs.")

Exercises F

1. In the examples below appear instances of *personification*, *simile*, *metaphor*, and *allusion*. Classify each instance.
   a. Joy is a partnership,
         Grief weeps alone;
      Many guests had Cana,
         Gethsemane had one.—Frederic Lawrence Knowles
   b. The Worldly Hope men set their Hearts upon
      Turns Ashes—or it prospers; and anon,
         Like Snow upon the Desert's dusty Face,
      Lighting a little hour or two—is gone.—Edward Fitzgerald

2. What is meant by the statement "*Comparison* as a *topic* seeks to discover meaningful likenesses"? Cite a topic or two that suits this purpose.

_3. What does the term *analogy* mean?

4. What is the purpose of analogy in *argumentation*? Can one *prove* anything by an analogy or only clarify a problem or suggest possibilities for investigation?

5. Provide an example of argument by analogy, one you have heard or originated.

6. Why do ministers often use "inspirational analogies" in their sermons?

7. What does the word *theorizing* mean? Of what value is analogy in theorizing?

8. Think of an analogy that would be or has been useful in theorizing, such as that used by Isaac Newton (apples and celestial bodies obey the same physical laws).

9. Think of a complex idea that *you* understand but that someone else in your class might not, and explain that idea by means of an analogy.

10. Your instructor may briefly explain one or two concepts such as those suggested by *tabula rasa; id, ego, and superego; cyclical theory of history;* Plato's *allegory of the cave;* M. H. Abrams' *the mirror and the lamp;* or Swift's *spider and bee*. Are such concepts analogies? Explain.

11. Your instructor may wish to make one or more of the following assignments:

    a. A *comparison* theme which stresses meaningful likenesses between two sets. (Suggested topics appear on pages 47–48: for *contrast*, simply read *compare*. Additional suggested topics appear on pages 66–67: for *compare and contrast* read *compare*.)

    b. A theme using analogy for argumentative purposes.*

    c. A theme using analogy for inspirational purposes.

    d. A theme using analogy for theorizing purposes.

    e. A theme using analogy for explanatory purposes.

---

*You will notice that we are not supplying suggested topics for analogy, though we have done so for other kinds of topics. The reason for this is that we cannot anticipate what two "frames of reference" ("chess and life," "a rock and human consciousness," "a bug and regeneration") may merge in your mind.

Compare-and-Contrast Topics

Comparison is rarely found in a pure state. If the sets to be compared were absolutely identical, there would, of course, be no need to compare them at all, since what we would say about one of those sets would automatically apply to the others as well. Since the sets we compare *are different*, if only in the degree of similarity of the elements being compared, *comparison* typically involves *contrast* as well. And what is true of *comparison* is also true of *contrast*. One can always find points of likeness in dissimilar sets, else there would be scarcely any purpose in distinguishing them. To refer to the specimen *contrast* theme on pages 41–42, Thomas Jefferson and Alexander Hamilton *did* have something in common—among other things, they both had a view of human nature and a conception of government. Likewise, to refer to *Example D* on page 40, Samuel Seabury, John Dickinson, and Thomas Paine did have something in common—among other things, an attitude toward the American Revolution. Hence, *contrast* typically involves *comparison* as well.

To write a *compare-and-contrast* theme or essay successfully is to demonstrate great powers of discrimination, command of the materials under one's purview, and a mastery of organization. As Emerson remarked, the human mind operates in two major ways: it finds similarities in difference and differences in similarity. The purpose in writing a *compare-and-contrast* theme is to discover meaningful likenesses *and* differences between two or more sets. One method of organizing *compare-and-contrast* themes appears in *Example A* below, although organization will vary somewhat according to the number of sets and elements involved.

**Example A:
One Way of Organizing COMPARE-AND-CONTRAST Themes**

First paragraph.
A thesis sentence asserting that S_1 and S_2 can be compared and contrasted in respect to four elements.

Second paragraph.
S_1 considered in respect to the four elements. (Since the four elements are members of S_1, they are, or ought to be, related and can be treated together. In this paragraph no attempt need be made to compare and contrast S_1 with S_2. The chief concern here is to present the evidence that will become the basis for comparison and contrast in paragraph three.)

Third paragraph.
S_2 considered in respect to the four elements, and how the elements of this set compare and contrast with the four elements of S_1.

Exercise A

The theme that appears below is designed to illustrate the form of organization discussed in *Example A* above. Analyze the theme by answering these questions.

1. Identify the two sets and each of their four elements.
2. What evidence is presented in paragraph 2 concerning the four elements of S_1?
3. What evidence is presented in paragraph 3 concerning the four elements of S_2?
4. What points of comparison and contrast are made between S_1 and S_2?

A COMPARE-AND-CONTRAST Theme Having Two Sets and Four Elements

HUCK FINN AND HOLDEN CAULFIELD*

The central characters of Mark Twain's *Adventures of Huckleberry Finn* and J. D. Salinger's *Catcher in the Rye* can be compared and contrasted in respect to their adolescence, their attempts to escape from repressive situations, the discoveries they make about humanity, and the insights they gain into themselves.

Huck Finn is a young man not yet inducted into adulthood. Because of this, Twain's novel is really a tale of initiation in which, typically, a young person is introduced to evil, in the process of which he gains wisdom at the cost of his innocence. Unable to endure the rigors of being "sivilized" by the Widow Douglas and Miss Watson—Huck had, for instance, to wear new clothes, mind his manners, respond robotlike to a dinner bell, listen to Bible readings, and say his prayers—Huck decides to run away. His adventures on land and on the Mississippi teach him a great deal at first hand: the pleasures of nature uncontaminated by corrupt human beings; the joy of friendship; the fact that Jim is a human being and, as such, is a living refutation of those laws that regard him merely as runaway property. But Huck's adventures also show him the moral rot in humanity. He sees Pap, whose only concerns seem to be liquor and getting his hands on Huck's "treasure." He sees the Duke and King, who live by their wits and prey upon others, even to using a corpse for their confidence game. He sees the Grangerfords and the Shepherdsons, who, as Christ-loving neighbors, devoutly kill each other, even after church services. He sees the lynch-mob, which appears to be courageous but which proves to be made up of abject cowards. He sees the "gallant" Colonel Sherburn, who prides himself upon his Southern code, a code that nevertheless impels him to kill the silly drunkard Boggs in cold blood. He sees the bounty hunters who search for fugitive slaves but who can hardly leave fast enough when Huck pretends that Jim has a contagious disease. Such people as these seem to be

*This theme was written by one of the authors to exemplify the principles under discussion.

living examples of the doctrine of innate depravity. Huck, of course, also finds evil in himself, something that is not the least of his discoveries. He finds that he is ingrained with some of the vicious prejudices of his community, and that he cannot run away from them as easily as he did from the Widow Douglas and Miss Watson. In this sense he finds he has much in common with the Grangerfords and the Shepherdsons and with Colonel Sherburn, for they too are vicious by reason of their prejudices. Similarly, Huck finds that he has much in common with the Duke and the King, for he also is forced to live by his wits, by deception—not, of course, for the purpose of preying upon others but of surviving in a world peopled by such folk. A dramatic example of this occurs when Huck, rationalizing his treachery, prepares to betray Jim, though they share a common plight and though Jim has proved of simple purity compared with the foulness of most of the people they encounter on their journey. But Huck, fortunately, has imagination and warmth of heart. Thus, he is able to anticipate what effect his act will have upon himself, let alone upon Jim, and he stops behaving like an automaton. In fact, he begins to purge himself of prejudice, though the process is realistically slow and Huck cannot help reverting to childish behavior from time to time.

Holden Caulfield, though also an adolescent, is not Huck Finn, though he too seeks to escape from a repressive situation and in time discovers something, not only about humanity, but about himself. Though as miserable at prep school as Huck was at the Widow Douglas home, his flight is not voluntary like Huck's, but forced, for he is a flunk-out. Compared with Huck's healthy sense of life, Holden's seems like that of a rat driven demented in a maze by some unseen experimenter. Huck seems to escape for positive reasons, because he feels smothered by the Widow Douglas and Pap and the community in general, whereas Holden seeks to escape for purely negative reasons. Holden's introduction to evil, it would seem, took place in some remote past, and though he has lost his innocence, he has gained little wisdom. The world, as he sees it, is phony, crappy, perverty, vomity-looking, and, above all, depressing, to use his favorite words. As Holden himself says, "I don't get hardly anything out of anything. . . . I'm in lousy shape." His trouble, as with Huck, is partly the world's fault, partly his own, but Huck, of course, is no psychological kin of Holden. Holden is squeamish to the point of being a casebook neurotic, easily bored, easily offended, easily made nervous, easily depressed, and easily made suicidal. For these reasons, unlike Huck, he is hardly able to cope with his world, as Huck manages to do, though as Mr. Antolini, his former English teacher, rightly remarks, he is "not the first person who was ever confused and frightened and even sickened by human behavior." Pency Prep, for example, is "about the fourth school" he has gone to, either flunking out or quitting. Holden, consequently, unlike Huck, feels a great pity for himself, a pity that expresses itself in fantasying. Senselessly, if amusingly, he tells a kindly disposed woman that he has "this tiny little tumor on the brain." At other times he imagines he has a bullet in his guts and that he is bleeding to death. His most "realistic" fantasy is that he will go out west to Huck Finn country, become a service station attendant, and pretend all the while that he is a deaf-mute—a sure symptom of withdrawal from a world with which he cannot cope. When he is not fantasying in this way, he identifies with children, for he is himself really a child, emotionally arrested as he is. Like Peter Pan, he is a boy who refuses to grow up. Too, as Peter Pan was to the "lost children," he wants to be a catcher in the rye. "I know it's crazy," he says, "but that's the only thing I'd really like to be." According to this fantasy, there would be thousands of children playing in a large field of rye and nobody else would be there ("nobody big, I mean") except himself, and he would catch any child that started to go over the cliff. Everyone seems to recognize this childishness, this refusal to grow up, in Holden, including himself. By his own account he acts as if he "was only about twelve," although the experiences he relates occurred when he was sixteen. Carl Luce, a former dorm mate, says to him, "when are you going to grow up?" and suggests that he see a psychoanalyst. Mr. Antolini has the sense to see that Holden is like those people who look "for something their . . . environment couldn't supply them with. Or they thought their own environment couldn't supply them with. So they gave up looking." And even his ten-year-old sister Phoebe tells him, "You don't like *anything* that's happening." Challenged by her, he thinks of what he does like: the two nuns whom he imagines to be going "around collecting dough in those beat-up straw baskets," though they are in fact schoolteachers; his younger brother Allie, now dead; and James Castle, a schoolmate of his who, abused by six of his fellow students, flung himself to death out of a window. It is not surprising, then, that Holden suffers a psychotic episode: he feels, in getting down curbs, that he might fall into an abyss and that he would "just go down, down, down, and nobody'd ever see me again." Thus, we find him telling his story in what seems to be a psychiatric ward, where, we hope, he will soon be able to view his experiences somewhat objectively, to recognize that the evil he has seen almost everywhere is partially, at least, the bleak projection of his own sickness, and that, far from being a catcher in the rye, he is in need of one. In this way, he may even come to be like Huck, vital, fundamentally happy, and fully alive.

To illustrate *compare-and-contrast* organization as clearly as possible, the above theme was printed as three paragraphs: the first consisting of the thesis sentence; the second of a discussion of S_1 and its four elements; and the third of S_2 and its four elements and how these four elements compare and contrast with the four elements of S_1. These paragraphs in their present form are much too long, a condition that can be remedied by reparagraphing the theme according to the analysis that follows.

Paragraph	Analysis
1	Thesis sentence
2	First two elements ("adolescence" and "attempts to escape from repressive situations") combined into one paragraph
3	Third element (Huck's "discoveries" about humanity)
4	Fourth element (Huck's "insights" into himself)
5	First three elements ("adolescence," "attempts to escape from repressive situations," and Holden's "discoveries" about humanity) combined into one paragraph.
6	Fourth element (Holden's "insights" into himself)

Various permutations in the organization of compare-and-contrast themes are both possible and acceptable. Again, organization will vary somewhat according to the number of sets and elements considered. Two such permutations appear in *Examples B* below.

Examples B: Permutations of the Organization of COMPARE-AND-CONTRAST Themes

First paragraph.
A thesis sentence asserting that S_1 and S_2 can be compared and contrasted in respect to two elements. (Huck and Holden can be compared and contrasted in respect to the discoveries they make about humanity and the insights they gain into themselves.)

Second paragraph.
S_1 and S_2 *compared* in respect to the first element. (Huck discovers evil in Pap, the Duke and the King, the Grangerfords and Shepherdsons, etc. Holden discovers evil in his teachers and classmates at Pencey Prep, in the bellboy, in Mr. Antolini, etc.)

Third paragraph.
S_1 and S_2 *contrasted* in respect to the first element. (Huck's discoveries about humanity enable him to mature and to cope with evil, etc. Holden's discoveries about humanity cause him to be overwhelmed by a sense of evil, to revert to childishness, to avoid entering the adult world, etc.)

Fourth paragraph.
S_1 and S_2 *compared* in respect to the second element. (Huck discovers evil in himself as well as in humanity and begins the slow process of ridding himself of its root, which is prejudice, etc. Holden, becoming more and more aware that the evil he sees in humanity may be largely the projection of his own sickness, finally begins the slow purgative process of retelling his experiences under the care of a psychiatrist, etc.)

Fifth paragraph.
S_1 and S_2 *contrasted* in respect to the second element. (Once Huck discovers evil in himself, he is able to mature by virtue of his own strength and judgment and thus becomes better able to cope with the world and himself, etc. Holden, however, does not mature by reason of his own strength and judgment. Instead, his discoveries about himself—that he cannot endure the real world, that his fantasies simply cannot be realized, that he is weak and self-pitying—finally prove shattering and cause him to seek, or be led to seek, a psychiatrist, who *may* help him to mature and to cope with the world and himself, etc.)

First paragraph.
A thesis sentence asserting that S_1 and S_2 can be compared and contrasted in respect to two elements. (Huck and Holden can be compared and contrasted in respect to the discoveries they make about humanity and about themselves.)

Second paragraph.
S_1 and S_2 *compared and contrasted* in respect to the first element. (Where Huck discovers evil in Pap, the Duke and the King, the Grangerfords and the Shepherdsons, etc., Holden discovers evil in his teachers and classmates at

Pency Prep, in the bellboy, in Mr. Antolini, etc. But where Huck's discoveries about humanity enable him to mature and to cope with evil, etc., Holden's discoveries about humanity cause him to be overwhelmed by a sense of evil, to revert to childishness, etc.)

Third paragraph.
S_1 and S_2 *compared and contrasted* in respect to the second element. (Huck also discovers evil in himself and begins the slow process of ridding himself of its root, which is prejudice, etc. Holden, similarly, becomes aware that there is evil, or at least sickness, in himself and finally begins the slow purgative process of retelling his experiences under the care of a psychiatrist, etc. Once Huck recognizes evil in himself, he is able to mature by virtue of his own strength and judgment. Holden, however, does not mature by reason of his own strength and judgment. Instead, his discoveries about himself finally prove shattering and cause him to seek, or be led to seek, a psychiatrist, who *may* help him to mature and to cope with world and himself, etc.)

Another permutation of the organization of *compare-and-contrast* themes is illustrated by the selection below, written by Samuel Johnson, one of the most disciplined writers of the English language. Dr. Johnson uses the word *genius* to mean *spirit*, as can be inferred from the context.

Exercises B   Analyze the following selection by answering these questions.

1. The thesis sentence has been omitted from the portion of the essay reprinted below. Reconstruct a thesis sentence from the paragraphs below.
2. Does Dr. Johnson treat the subject as a *why* or *what* topic? Explain.
3. Identify the element compared and contrasted in each of the paragraphs.
4. Formulate by symbolic notation the organization of this selection.

JOHN DRYDEN AND ALEXANDER POPE

In acquired knowledge the superiority must be allowed [not to Pope but] to Dryden, whose education was more scholastick, and who before he became an author had been allowed more time for study, with better means of information. His mind has a larger range, and he collects his images and illustrations from a more extensive circumference of science. Dryden knew more of man in his general nature, and Pope in his local manners. The notions of Dryden were formed by comprehensive speculation, and those of Pope by minute attention. There is more dignity in the knowledge of Dryden, and more certainty in that of Pope.

Poetry was not the sole praise of either, for both excelled likewise in prose; but Pope did not borrow his prose from his predecessor [Dryden]. The style of Dryden is capricious and varied, that of Pope is cautious and uniform; Dryden obeys the motions of his own mind, Pope constrains his mind to his own rules of composition. Dryden is sometimes vehement and rapid; Pope is always smooth, uniform, and gentle. Dryden's page is a natural field, rising into inequalities, and diversified by the varied exuberance of abundant vegetation; Pope's is a velvet lawn, shaven by the scythe, and levelled by the roller.

Of genius, that power which constitutes a poet; that quality without which judgement is cold and knowledge is inert; that energy which collects, combines, amplifies, and animates—the superiority must, with some hesitation, be allowed to Dryden. It is not to be inferred that of this poetical vigour Pope had only a little, because Dryden had more, for every writer since Milton must give place to Pope; and even of Dryden it must be said that if he has brighter paragraphs, he has not better poems. Dryden's performances were always hasty, either excited by some external occasion, or extorted by domestick necessity; he composed without consideration, and published without correction. What his mind could supply at call, or gather in one excursion, was all that he sought, and all that he gave. The dilatory caution of Pope enabled him to condense his sentiments, to multiply his images, and to accumulate all that study might produce, or chance might supply. If the flights of Dryden therefore are higher, Pope continues longer on the wing. If of Dryden's fire the blaze is brighter, of Pope's the heat is more regular and constant. Dryden often surpasses expectation, and Pope never falls below it. Dryden is read with frequent astonishment, and Pope with perpetual delight.—From "Alexander Pope" in *Lives of the English Poets* by Samuel Johnson.

A Selection Illustrating the Use of Analogy for COMPARISON AND CONTRAST

Compare-and-contrast themes may be based upon analogy in order to make the unknown known, the complex simple, the unfamiliar familiar. The selection below illustrates this idea. In this excerpt from Mark Twain's *The Mysterious Stranger*, an angel who has taken human form is trying to explain to a boy that he has nothing in common with human beings. To make his explanation clear, the angel *contrasts* an elephant and a spider, in the process of which he *compares* himself to the elephant and man to the spider. Then, by applying the findings of his analogy, the angel *compares and contrasts* himself with man. You will notice that, though Twain does not follow a rigid system of paragraphing, he nevertheless has a thesis sentence.

In this paragraph the angel contrasts an elephant and a spider, likening himself to the elephant and man to the spider.

OF ANGELS AND MEN

"Men have nothing in common with me. . . . I will show you what I mean. Here is a red spider, not so big as a pin's head. Can you imagine an elephant being interested in him—caring whether he is happy or isn't, or whether he is wealthy or poor, or whether his sweetheart returns his love or not, or whether his mother is sick or well, or whether he is looked up to in society or not, or whether his enemies will smite him or his friends desert him, or whether his hopes will suffer blight or his political ambitions fail, or whether he shall die in the bosom of his family or neglected and despised in a foreign land? These things can never be important to the elephant, they are nothing to him, he cannot shrink his sympathies to the microscopic size of them. Man is to me as the red spider is to the elephant. The elephant has nothing against the spider—he cannot get down to that remote level; I have nothing against man. The elephant is indifferent; I am indifferent. The elephant would not take the trouble to do the spider an ill turn; if he took the notion he might do him a good turn, if it came in his way and cost nothing. I have done men good service but no ill turns.

In this paragraph the angel draws an analogical conclusion: "man is immeasurably further below me than is the wee spider below the elephant."

"The elephant lives a century, the red spider a day; in power, intellect, and dignity the one creature is separated from the other by a distance which is simply astronomical. Yet in these, as in all qualities, man is immeasurably further below me than is the wee spider below the elephant.

In this paragraph the angel compares and contrasts himself to man in respect to their creative powers.

"Man's mind clumsily and tediously and laboriously patches little trivialities together and gets a result—such as it is. My mind creates! Do you get the force of that? Creates anything it desires—and in a moment. Creates without material. Creates fluids, solids, colors—anything, everything—out of the airy nothing which is called Thought. A man imagines a silk thread, imagines a machine to make it, imagines a picture, then by weeks of labor embroiders it on canvas with the thread. I think the whole thing, and in a moment it is before you—created. . . .

In this paragraph the angel, applying his analogy, compares and contrasts himself with man.

"Now, then, I perceive by your thoughts that you are understanding me fairly well. Let us proceed. Circumstances might so fall out that the elephant could like the spider—supposing he can see it—but he could not love it. His love is for his own kind—for his equals. An angel's love is sublime, adorable, divine, beyond the imagination of man—infinitely beyond it! But it is limited to his own august order. If it fell upon one of your race for only an instant, it would consume its object to ashes. No, we cannot love men but we can be harmlessly indifferent to them."—From Mark Twain's *The Mysterious Stranger*.

Exercise C

Write a *compare-and-contrast* theme of about one thousand words. Below appear some suggested topics. To make clear sense of these topics, assume that the expression "Compare and contrast" appears before each of them. For additional topics see *"Suggested CONTRAST Topics"* (pages 47–48), which can readily be converted into *compare-and-contrast* topics.

Suggested Topics for COMPARE-AND-CONTRAST Themes

1. Two novels (such as Aldous Huxley's *Brave New World* and George Orwell's *1984*)
2. Two plays (such as Clifford Odets' *Waiting for Lefty* and Samuel Beckett's *Waiting for Godot*; or Aeschylus' Agamemnon trilogy and Eugene O'Neill's *Mourning Becomes Electra*)
3. A book with its source (such as Archibald MacLeish's *J. B.* and the Book of Job in the Old Testament)
4. Two characters (such as Captain Ahab in Herman Melville's *Moby-Dick* and King Ahab in the Old Testament)
5. A book with its movie version (such as Dostoevski's *Crime and Punishment*, Nelson Algren's *The Man with the Golden Arm*, Walter Van Tilburg Clark's *The Oxbow Incident*, or Margaret Mitchell's *Gone with the Wind*)
6. Two humorists (such as Mark Twain and James Thurber)
7. Two cartoonists (such as Herblock and Mauldin)

8. Two poems (such as John Keats' "Ode to a Nightingale" and "Ode on a Grecian Urn")
9. Two historical figures (such as Gen. Ulysses S. Grant and Gen. Robert E. Lee; or William Lloyd Garrison and John Brown)
10. Two minority groups (such as Cubans and Puerto Ricans)
11. Two concepts (such as *Pelagianism* and *Augustinianism*; *state of nature* and *civil society*; *natural rights* and *civil rights*)
12. Two religions (such as Anglicanism and Catholicism; Congregationalism and Presbyterianism)
13. Two planets (such as Jupiter and Saturn)
14. Socialism and communism (or any two related concepts in physics, chemistry, psychology, etc.)
15. Formal and informal education
16. Liberal and technical education
17. Two classic experiments
18. Henry David Thoreau and Jean-Paul Sartre as existentialists
19. Passive resistance as used by Martin Luther King, Jr., and Mohandas Gandhi
20. The human mind and the "mind" of an electronic computer
21. Charles Darwin's and Alfred Russell Wallace's theories of evolution
22. Journalism and literature
23. Christopher Columbus and Amerigo Vespucci (or any other two explorers)
24. Charles Proteus Steinmetz and Thomas Alva Edison (or Johannes Kepler and Isaac Newton)
25. Two musical instruments (or the human voice and a musical instrument)
26. Two novelists (such as Ernest Hemingway and Sherwood Anderson; William Faulkner and Erskine Caldwell)
27. Science and art (or science and religion)
28. Two wars (such as the French and American revolutions; the Korean and Vietnam wars)
29. The United Nations and the League of Nations
30. Franklin Delano Roosevelt's "New Deal" and Lyndon B. Johnson's "The Great Society"

The **What-What-Why** Topic and Its Variations

Contrast topics, *comparison* topics, and *compare-and-contrast* topics require us to use either *what* sets or *why* sets, but do not allow us to combine *what* and *why* sets. For this reason we have the *what-what-why* topic, which enables us to use such a combination. This kind of topic, which involves research, is usually reserved for long term papers inasmuch as the paper fundamentally consists of three interrelated essays on the same topic.

The *what-what-why* topic has a threefold purpose: to enable us to present authoritative opinions and ascertained facts concerning the positive and negative sides of an issue and to draw our own opinions from the evidence presented. That being the case, each of the three sections of the paper is governed by its own thesis sentence—the first and second sections by *what* thesis sentences (*S* contains *a . . . v*) and the third section by a *why* thesis sentence (*S* because of *l . . . n*).

Suppose, for instance, that you are concerned with the issue of capital punishment and wish to investigate the facts and opinions that make this subject so controversial. Suppose too that, having collected and organized your findings (the facts and opinions in the case), you now wish to present, not only your findings, but your own opinion as well. Given your threefold intention, you would devote about one-third of your paper to elaborating the thesis sentence: "The subset of facts and opinions opposing capital punishment can be represented by *a . . . v*." Having accomplished this, you would turn to the second section of your paper, devoting another third of your space to elaborating the second thesis sentence: "The subset of facts and opinions favoring capital punishment can be represented by *a . . . v*." (Whether you begin your paper with a discussion of the positive or negative elements is a matter of judgment, but the section dealing with your own opinion always remains the final section.)

Once you have *fairly* presented the crucial facts and opinions concerning the case against and for capital punishment (a fairness further evidenced by the more or less equal space you accord both positions), you are ready to present your own opinion, which becomes an elaboration of the thesis sentence, "The laws governing capital punishment should be abolished (retained, modified) because of *l . . . n*." Inasmuch as your opinion is the climax of your paper, you should discuss it fully to the point where it is on a par with your other discussions. (A model theme exemplifying this three-part organization of a *what-what-why* topic appears below.)

Other combinations of the *what-what-why* form are possible in order to answer *what-what* topics and *what-why* topics. The *what-what* topic (e.g., What is the evidence for *and* against a given position?) is obviously designed for a two-part rather than a three-part paper because it does not call for an opinion. The *what-why* topic (e.g., What is the evidence for *or* against a given position and what is your opinion?) is again obviously designed for a two-part paper, but instead of your opinion being omitted, either the positive or negative side of the question is omitted.

Exercises A

1. Identify the topics below that call for a one-part, two-part, or three-part paper:
    a. The case for and against Adolf Eichmann and my opinion
    b. The case against professional boxing
    c. The case for the conspiracy theory in the assassination of President John F. Kennedy and my opinion
    d. The case for and against euthanasia
    e. The case for nationalization of the American railway system and my opinion
    f. The case for and against the South in the American Civil War
2. In studying the following theme, which is a model of a three-part paper on a *what-what-why* topic, point out the three thesis sentences and identify each of them as a *what* or *why* thesis sentence.
3. Point out the elements of each thesis sentence.
4. Explain whether the paragraphs that succeed each thesis sentence follow in an orderly sequence.
5. What is the topic of each paragraph that is not a thesis sentence?
6. How has the writer arranged his elements? Has he used *random arrangement*, *partially random arrangement*, *climactic arrangement*, *chronological arrangement*, or *partially chronological arrangement*?
7. Explain whether the evidence cited in this paper is sufficient to strengthen your convictions if you are an "abolitionist," or weaken your convictions if you are an "anti-abolitionist."

Model Theme on a WHAT-WHAT-WHY Topic

THE CASE AGAINST AND FOR CAPITAL PUNISHMENT AND MY VERDICT*

The case against capital punishment rests upon five main points: the death penalty does not deter potential criminals from committing major crimes; the sensationalism aroused by a capital crime prejudices the cause of justice; criminals are not treated equally before the law; sometimes innocent people are executed; and, finally, the principle of talion, summed up as an eye for an eye, is a barbarism in a civilized world.

Those who want to abolish capital punishment (a punishment restored by the Supreme Court in 1976, though, in an earlier decision, the same court had

*This is a student term paper that has been edited by the authors. Your instructor may call for full citations of your sources of information, and he may want those citations to appear at the foot of the page or at the end of the theme instead of in the body of the theme.

outlawed it as "cruel and unusual punishment") contend that the death penalty does not deter criminals to any determinable degree. "Abolitionist" sociologists, for instance, report that homicide rates in states that refused to apply the death penalty were about the same as in neighboring states that invoked the death penalty (statistics based, of course, on equal population figures). For instance, Massachusetts, then a "death" state, was compared with Rhode Island, then a "life" state, for a total of sixteen years (the years between 1940 and 1955). Homicide rates, it turned out, were higher for Massachusetts in seven of the years, and Rhode Island's lower in the other nine. This is powerful evidence that so-called capital crimes—crimes that have included rape, kidnapping, armed robbery, murder, and treason—are not halted by the threat of the death penalty. Some abolitionist psychologists argue against the death penalty on different grounds. One of their leading contentions is that a person often commits murder from an urge to destroy himself. In other words, they see murder as a twisted way of courting suicide. Some criminologists oppose the death penalty for any crime other than murder because, they contend, a remediable crime often leads to an irremediable one. For instance, in states where kidnapping, or rape, or armed robbery had warranted the death penalty, the criminal risked nothing in murdering his victim. In fact, he stood to gain a great deal. He got rid of a witness and thus minimized the possibility of being detected and executed. A classic example of the ineffectiveness of capital punishment as a deterrent occurred in nineteenth-century England where a pickpocket was busily plying his trade in front of a gallows while a friend of his was being hanged for picking pockets. A more recent story is told about an Ohio man, Charlie Justice by name, who, while in prison, designed the clamps which hold a man in an electric chair. Shortly after he was paroled, Justice was back in jail waiting to be electrocuted for killing a man. Likewise, Alfred Wells who helped install the gas chamber at San Quentin died in the same chamber four years later.

If capital punishment can be condemned as a deterrent, it can also be condemned for encouraging maladministration of justice. When a person commits a capital crime, the pretrial and trial period becomes sensationalized by newspapers, television, radio, and by word of mouth. The reactions of the public, thus powerfully aroused and manipulated, fuse into a massive force that cannot help entering the courtroom and influencing justice. Consciously or unconsciously, prospective jurors are bound to be influenced by such incendiary feelings, whatever disclaimers they may make to the contrary. Nor can the lawyers or even the judge in the case be entirely immune to such contagion. In ways difficult to detect but that nevertheless are operative, such sensationalism does affect the testimony of witnesses, the attitudes of lawyers, the decisions of the judge on points of procedure, and, of course, the crucial verdict of the jury.

The third point that abolitionists cite is the matter of equality before the law. Because there is no infallible way to determine just when the death penalty should be invoked, the judge and sometimes the jury are given the power to decide. As has already been pointed out, the power of journalism or even of local mores is such that it can move a prosecuting attorney to demand the death penalty, or influence a judge's instructions to a jury, or warp the verdict of the jury as well. In Southern states, for example, blacks were almost invariably executed when found guilty of murdering a white man or of raping a white woman. If, however, a black murdered another black or raped a black woman, the sentence was seldom death. According to *Newsweek* of February 11, 1963, ''more than half of the 3,800 persons executed in the U.S. since 1930 were Negroes''—a figure so disproportionate that it proclaims the fact that inequality before the law is the rule and not the exception. Similarly, two California men named Thomas and McCain killed a person while committing robbery. Thomas was tried before a judge and was executed. McCain was tried by a jury and received life imprisonment. According to the *Newsweek* article cited, of thirty-two persons executed in Missouri, thirty-one had filed appeals as ''poor persons.'' Such evidence, to repeat, is sufficient to prove that equality before the law is an ideal, not a reality.

The fourth argument that abolitionists advance has its basis in the fact that people are occasionally put to death for crimes they did not commit. When such a tragedy occurs and the innocence of the executed person is established, nothing can be done to restore that person to life. Neither can anything be done to relieve his shocked family and friends. In such instances the law as murderer is exposed in its most brutal form, and people cannot help but lose respect for its alleged majesty. During the course of a single year, according to an article in the *Rotarian* of May 1959, four men in California were executed and later proved innocent. In New Jersey over a twenty-five-year period, fifteen innocent persons were killed by due process. These examples, of course, represent only a few of known or knowable cases. If capital punishment were outlawed and life imprisonment substituted as the penalty for the most serious crimes, society could be protected from the murderer on the one hand and, no less importantly, from the crime of being a murderer itself.

The last important abolitionist argument is that we supposedly live in a civilized world where there is no place for the barbaric law of talion that demands an eye for an eye, a tooth for a tooth, and a murder for a murder. If murder is an atrocious and unpardonable act for one man, it is no less atrocious, no less unpardonable, for a mass of men. Indeed, done by cold-blooded and allegedly sane court procedure and under the majesty of the law, it is, if anything, an even greater atrocity and infinitely less pardonable. Those who commit crimes, whether so-called capital ones or other kinds, have the right to become rehabilitated and, in time and when possible, to become valuable members of society again. Nathan Leopold is only one example of the truth of this statement and his case, though famous, is by no means exceptional. According to *Life* magazine of May 9, 1960, it is the rule and not the exception that paroled murderers often lead normal lives. For example, in California, out of ''342 prisoners convicted of first degree murder and paroled between 1945 and 1954, only nine had been returned to prison on a new felony conviction by June 30, 1956.''

II

The case for retaining capital punishment rests largely upon the principle of deterrence and a rebuttal of the four points already discussed.

The argument that the death penalty is a powerful deterrent is one that, in the eyes of the anti-abolitionists, makes all other considerations unimportant or merely sophistical. They say that in states where capital punishment exists, a person who contemplates robbery, for example, will hesitate to take a weapon with him lest he might kill and be executed in consequence. Abolish the death penalty again, remove that fear, and we not only encourage criminals of every stripe to carry lethal weapons but to use them as well. It is fear, they say, fear of the noose, of the electric chair, of the gas chamber, that often makes the crucial difference between robbery, say, and robbery-*cum*-murder. They point out that in England the principle of deterrence has sunk so deeply into the consciousness of Englishmen that policemen do not carry guns at all. Moreover, in states that impose the death penalty, murder is still held to be the "king of crimes." By abolishing the death penalty, we abolish the very fear that keeps untold murders, kidnappings, and rapes from occurring, statistics for which cannot be gathered even by experts in criminal statistics.

Anti-abolitionists agree with abolitionists that the cause of justice is sometimes unduly swayed by journalistic sensationalism; but *that*, they feel, is the price we pay for a free press. More to the point, they contend that so long as justice is administered by human agency, it cannot be pure—that error, whether of a trivial or significant nature, is bound to occur, with or without sensationalism. If the possibility that injustice may occur in our courts is to be taken as a sound objection to court procedure, we would have to scrap our entire legal machinery. The fact, therefore, that injustice does occasionally occur is of far less importance than the fact that justice is dispensed and dispensed equitably for the most part.

By the same token, anti-abolitionists also agree that there is inequality before the law—that men, who are convicted of the same crime may be given unequal sentences—one life imprisonment, for instance, the other death. But inequality, they feel, is no justification for discontinuing the death penalty. The real issue is that those who commit capital crimes be executed. That some persons who commit capital crimes escape death is, admittedly, unfair. But if unfairness is an objection, abolitionists should insist with anti-abolitionists that the death penalty be imposed in all fifty states. For a murderer in a "life" state is obviously given preferential treatment compared to that dispensed a murderer in a "death" state. But here again it can be insisted that absolute equality before the law is an ideal, not a reality. If we are to abolish capital punishment because of the possibility of inequality, then in all fairness we must abolish entirely the practice of pronouncing sentence upon anyone and thus scrap our whole legal system in the bargain. The trouble with abolitionists, they contend, is perfectionism. If they cannot have absolutely perfect law perfectly executed, they want none at all. They deceive themselves—and others—into thinking they are humanitarians when, actually, they are anti-humanitarians, since they seem to prefer no law to bad law.

As for the charge that innocent people are sometimes executed, anti-abolitionists argue that such instances are very rare, for our legal system is designed to minimize that risk, a risk, however, that in the nature of things we must accept. That is why a trial for a capital crime is so drawn out, why verdicts can be appealed to a higher and still higher court, and why governors have the prerogative up to the very moment of execution to defer or commute the death sentence. The purpose of law is to protect the rights and lives of citizens, and, given the human factor, the occasional execution of an innocent person is unfortunate and perhaps even unavoidable. But again, the fact that a system does not function perfectly is no reason to abandon it.

Finally, the argument that criminals deserve the opportunity to become rehabilitated does not mean that all of them will or can be rehabilitated. Of those who appear to be reformed and who are paroled, any one of them may kill again. One need scarcely cite the numbers who reappear in prisons as repeaters. Unless we are more concerned with the fate of murderers than with the lives of decent citizens, the death penalty must be retained.

III

After sifting the evidence for and against abolition, I favor outlawing capital punishment because, in contrast to the abolitionists, anti-abolitionists are on treacherous logical and moral ground.

First, they ignore statistical proof—the only kind of proof available or even applicable in the circumstances—that when certain states revoked the death penalty—e.g., Alaska, Hawaii, Maine, Michigan, Minnesota, North Dakota, Oregon, Rhode Island, and Wisconsin—the ratio of capital crimes to population did not increase on the average. Moreover, they ignore the fact that neighboring states, one a "death" state, the other a "life" state, have over a period of time the same frequency of capital crimes in relation to population. Their principal argument, then, that the death penalty is a deterrent cannot stand against such statistical assault. Furthermore, the question of justice that the abolitionists advance is warped by the anti-abolitionists. Abolitionists, however extreme, do not urge that we do away with our legal apparatus. Their only major objection to the law as it now stands is that it imposes the death penalty for certain crimes. They have no objection to life imprisonment, a sentence from which innocent persons can be released, or under which a man like Nathan Leopold can be rehabilitated, and one that reaffirms rather than denies the value of human life.

Capital punishment is founded on merely ethical norms, not on moral or religious grounds. Men are banded together into societies. There are in each of these societies normative ethics prescribing how we ought to behave in given circumstances. There is nothing permanent or universal or sacred about such norms, as witness the fact that within a few short years the Supreme Court has reversed itself entirely on the death penalty. Under such normative ethics, Germany attempted to exterminate its entire Jewish population as well as the Jewish populations of conquered countries. Under such normative ethics, many whites in our own country once held blacks to be chattel property and even received the sanction of the Supreme Court in the Dred Scott decision. Under such normative ethics, the electric chair was used in twenty-three of our states, not to mention the District of Columbia, the gas chamber in eleven, the noose in seven; and in Utah the condemned were given the choice of death by hanging or death by the firing squad. But there are moral rather than merely ethical norms, norms that are permanent, universal, and sacred. Such a norm was affirmed by Christ when He said that we must love one another and by Saint Augustine when he wrote, "First love, then do whatever you please." Were human life held sacred instead of cheapened by legal murder, we might all from childhood up be inculcated with this sense of the holiness of life. It is even conceivable under such circumstances that the violent would refrain from brutal acts like murder. But if the law has little respect for life, if the law refuses to set the example, it follows that not all citizens living under that law will. In any event, if murder is indeed evil and unpardonable, murder by law is no less so.

Suggested WHAT-WHAT, WHAT-WHY, and WHAT-WHAT-WHY Topics*

1. Birth control
2. The sale of arms abroad by the United States
3. The recent troubles in Northern Ireland
4. Collective bargaining for teachers
5. Abortion
6. The feminist movement
7. The atomic bombing of Hiroshima and Nagasaki in World War II
8. National Health Insurance
9. John Brown
10. The Nuremberg trials
11. Forced retirement
12. The CIA (FBI)
13. Unconditional amnesty for Vietnam deserters
14. Sen. Joseph McCarthy
15. Price supports for tobacco
16. On making Alaska a national park
17. The volunteer army
18. Lobbying
19. America's role in the Mexican War of 1846
20. The oil cartel
21. Gun laws
22. The censoring of books
23. Right of public officials to strike
24. A Supreme Court verdict
25. Professional boxing
26. The Gay Liberation Movement
27. Israel
28. Euthanasia
29. Federal aid to big cities
30. Cuba
31. School integration
32. Eugene V. Debs
33. Open marriages
34. Ku Klux Klan
35. X-rated movies
36. Social welfare
37. Present rape laws
38. No-fault insurance (divorce)
39. Cohabitation
40. Sensitivity groups

*If these topics are to be used for a two-part paper, reword them to read either: (1) The case for and against X; (2) The case for X and my opinion; or (3) The case against X and my opinion. If these topics are to be used for a three-part paper, simply reword them to read: The case for and against X and my opinion.

2 The Development of Paragraphs and the Nature of Evidence

Fact Statements

The strategies of organization discussed in the first section of this book are only a means of presenting information or opinion plus information in a non-random and intelligible form. By themselves alone these strategies of organization cannot make our information credible or our opinions persuasive, let alone intellectually irresistible. That achievement, if it is to be accomplished, must be done painstakingly, paragraph by paragraph, with each paragraph demonstrating the credibility of our information or the soundness of our opinions. **This process is called paragraph development.** If we are successful in developing our paragraphs, we shall persuade our readers that our information is reliable and our opinions creditable.

Paragraph Development and Evidence

To solve the problem of paragraph development, we have to distinguish various kinds of statements typically found in the body of themes. (*Body* designates everything in a theme that is neither a thesis nor summary.) These various kinds are (1) *fact statements*,* simple and compound, which may include statistics and opinions,† quoted or paraphrased, from pertinent sources; (2) *logic statements*, which serve as bridges from fact statement to fact statement, from fact statement to opinion statement, and from fact statement to opinion statement to opinion statement (see page 87); (3) *opinion statements* of our own; (4) *example statements* to explain an idea or point of view, to support an assertion, or to make an otherwise vague idea or point of view vivid, colorful, or forceful; and (5) *definition statements* whose function is orientative and explanatory. (There are, of course, other kinds of statements such as "Ouch!" that we shall ignore, since these are not the kinds that typically appear in themes and essays.)

The kinds of statements we have identified represent what is called *evidence* for topic sentences. Topic sentences are derived from the specified elements in the thesis sentence and constitute the controlling ideas of paragraphs. In

*The phrase "true facts" is obviously tautological; the phrase "false facts" is obviously self-contradictory; hence, the term *fact statements*, of which one can properly say, "This is a true fact statement," or "This is a false fact statement."
†The reason for cited opinions being classed as fact statements is explained in the footnotes to pp. 4 and 21.

short, the topic sentence is to the paragraph what the thesis sentence is to the entire theme.

When the topic sentence is supported by accurate, sufficient, and relevant evidence, we say that the paragraph is properly developed. In writing a paragraph, then, the writer is done the moment he judges the evidence to be such that it will convince any reasonable reader of the soundness of the topic sentence. To do less is to leave the point of the topic sentence in doubt; to do more is to belabor the point.

Simple Fact Statements

A *simple fact statement* does two things: (1) it describes a *single* natural phenomenon or a *single* historical event, and (2) it implies that the description is accurate or true. By a *natural phenomenon* we mean a natural event or a natural law, such as the eruption of an earthquake or the law of gravitation, over which man has little or no control. By an *historical* event we mean an occurrence in which man has played a significant role. An historical event can be as momentous as the splitting of the atom or the passage of the Bill of Rights, or as commonplace as an individual's birthplace or his grade-point average.

It may occur to the reader at this point that an *apparently* single event (such as one's birth) consists of a complex of both natural and historical events. This point is considered under *compound fact statements* (page 80). For the moment it is sufficient to point out that a complex of events can be anatomized into single (simple) fact statements.

Simple fact statements are called simple because they describe single phenomena or events. These statements, therefore, are two-valued because they are either true or false, never "in between." In other words, simple fact statements are two-value statements because they are either entirely correct or entirely incorrect, not half right or half wrong or partly right or partly wrong.

Since fact statements are descriptions of natural phenomena and historical events, we can determine whether those descriptions are indeed true by checking the phenomenon or event described. If there is no conceivable way of proving or disproving a fact statement in the present state of human knowledge, we shall have to conclude that we are not dealing with a fact statement as we may have supposed but with another kind of statement called *opinion statement*.

We said earlier that a *cited* opinion (another person's opinion that we quote or paraphrase) belongs to the class of fact statements (true or false) for the reason that the person is asserted to have expressed the opinion. Thus, as with any historical event, the assertion can be checked. It is a true fact statement that Walt Whitman expressed the opinion, "whoever walks a furlong without sympathy walks to his own funeral drest in his shroud." It is a false fact statement that Walt Whitman expressed the opinion that a "man of genius has been seldom ruined but by himself."

Below appear examples of simple fact statements.

Examples A:
Simple Fact Statements

1. This ball weighs six ounces.
2. Charles A. Lindbergh was an aviator.
3. I am presently a college student.

4. That is my Chevrolet.
5. My social security number is 123456789.
6. The Duke of Wellington said, "Nothing except a battle lost can be half so melancholy as a battle won.'
7. Gustave Flaubert observed that what is beautiful is moral.
8. The earth rotates.
9. Vesuvius erupted.

Exercises A

1. What is meant by *historical event*? By *natural phenomenon*? What is the plural form of *phenomenon*? Provide one or two examples of your own to illustrate your definition of *historical event* and *natural phenomenon*.
2. Explain why each of the statements in *Examples A* above is a fact statement? (*Example*: The statement about the ball weighing six ounces is a fact statement because it describes a natural phenomenon and implies that the statement is true—an accurate description, in other words, of a natural phenomenon.)
3. Explain how you would check each of those statements if you doubted their accuracy. (*Example*: In respect to the ball, I would weigh it.)
4. What is meant by the expression *two-value statement*?
5. Examine the fact statements above and determine which of those statements are indeed two-value statements.
6. What is a *cited* opinion? Why do cited opinions belong to the class of fact statements?
7. We said that if you encounter a fact statement (e.g., "Cancer is caused by a virus") that cannot yet be proved or disproved, you should consider it an opinion statement. Explain.

To check the accuracy of fact statements, you must, as you discovered, do something *physical*, such as consulting a physicist, a world almanac, or the registrar's records.

Simple fact statements, then, have four characteristics by which they can be identified. Put in the form of a thesis sentence, the definition of a simple fact statement reads: **A simple fact statement is a description of a single natural phenomenon or a single historical event, an assertion that the description is correct, an observation that can be checked physically, and a declaration that proves to be entirely true or entirely false.**

False Fact Statements

Not every assertion that a person makes is necessarily true, even if he intends to be honest. A person, for instance, may make the "honest mistake" of saying that the Civil War began in 1863 or that the cypress tree never loses its leaves. By the same token **a fact statement is not necessarily true; it only implies that it is an accurate description of a natural phenomenon or an historical event.**

Below are some examples of simple fact statements that were widely believed to be true at one time or another.

Examples B:
False Fact Statements

1. The father has nothing to do with the sex of his offspring.
2. The earth is flat.
3. An atom is the smallest particle of matter.
4. One gets warts from handling toads.
5. Witches can fly on broomsticks.
6. The Declaration of Independence was written entirely by Thomas Jefferson alone.
7. American Indians are indigenous to America.
8. The sun revolves around the earth.
9. Manure produces flies (an example of the theory of spontaneous generation).

Exercises B

1. The statements in *Examples B* above are simple fact statements. Explain.
2. How would you prove the inaccuracy of each of those statements?
3. We said that a topic sentence must be supported by accurate, sufficient, and relevant evidence. What is meant by *sufficient* fact statements? (If a district attorney argued in court that the accused was guilty of shooting another man on the grounds that a gun was found in his house, and it could be certified beyond doubt that the said gun was indeed found in the accused's house, would that be *sufficient* evidence for a jury to find the accused guilty of murder? If you were on the jury, what other factual evidence would you want?)
4. What is meant by *relevant* fact statements? (If a defense attorney argued in court that the accused could not have committed the murder because he was married and had three children, and these statements were verified, would you regard them as *relevant*? Explain.)
5. What effect is likely to be produced in a reader by false fact statements? By insufficient fact statements? By irrelevant fact statements?
6. Write three true simple fact statements of your own and label them: Three True Simple Fact Statements.
7. Write three false simple fact statements of your own and label them: Three False Simple Fact Statements.

Compound Fact Statements

Fact statements very often contain more than one description of natural phenomena or historical events, and even combine such occurrences (e.g., "In 1927 Charles A. Lindbergh, known as the Flyin' Fool and later as the Lone Eagle, made the first solo west-to-east flight across the Atlantic Ocean in a single-engined plane called 'The Spirit of St. Louis.' His flight from New York to Paris took him 33 hours and 39 minutes, and won him a prize of $25,000"). Since such a combination of fact statements cannot be called simple, we shall call them *compound*. Compound fact statements have all the characteristics of simple fact statements except that they are three-valued: they are either entirely accurate, entirely inaccurate, or partly inaccurate.

Exercises C:
Analyzing Compound
Fact Statements

Which of the statements below are (1) entirely accurate, (2) entirely inaccurate, or (3) partly inaccurate?

1. The sun is the center of our planetary system, and Mars is the planet farthest from the sun.
2. Madison is the capital of Kentucky, and Springfield is the capital of Illinois.
3. The French Revolution began in 1066, the same year that Columbus discovered America.
4. Oliver Cromwell was general of the Puritan forces in England when Charles II was beheaded, whereupon Cromwell became lord protector of England.
5. The first European settlers in the New World were the Spanish, who conquered the Indians they found there or caused them to flee for their lives.
6. Jimmy Carter, a Northern Episcopalian preacher, was elected president of the United States in 1976.

Before checking the accuracy of compound fact statements, one needs to anatomize them into simple fact statements. Thus, to take an obvious example, we would anatomize the statement "The French Revolution began in 1066, the same year that Columbus discovered America" into two simple fact statements: (1) The French Revolution began in 1066, and (2) Columbus discovered America in 1066. Then, either by the knowledge we already possess or by reference to a world history book, we would declare both statements to be false fact statements. Or, to shape our verdict more precisely, we would declare that this compound fact statement is entirely false for the reason that the French Revolution began in 1789, not 1066, and that Columbus discovered America in 1492, not 1066.

To consider another obvious example, we would anatomize the fact statement "Madison is the capital of Kentucky, and Springfield is the capital of Illinois" into two simple fact statements, declaring the first to be false, the second to be true, and the compound fact statement, therefore, only partly true because Madison is the capital of Wisconsin and Frankfort is the capital of Kentucky.

To consider something less obvious: To say that you *feel*, or *think*, or *believe* a fact statement to be true or false does not convert it into a true or false fact statement, any more than feeling, thinking, or believing you are a millionaire necessarily makes you one. All you do when you add such an expression as "I believe" to a *simple* fact statement is to convert it into a *compound* fact statement which, in turn, has to be reduced to two simple fact statements. To say, for instance, "I believe that a Russian was the first man on the moon" is to utter a compound fact statement consisting of (1) I believe the fact statement to be true that (2) a Russian was the first man on the moon. The first statement may indeed be true, just as the second statement is indeed false; but since fact statements are the heart of the problem, not one's psychological states in regard to them, the statement about one's belief or disbelief should be withheld on the grounds that it is irrelevant and complicates the problem unnecessarily. If, on the other hand, as was said, the accuracy of a fact statement cannot be proved or disproved in the present state of human knowledge, then we may say, "I think (feel, believe) this opinion to be sound (or unsound)," for the opinion has not yet passed into the class of fact statements.

The history of scholarship is the conversion of opinion statements into fact statements. (See the discussion of Ignaz Philipp Semmelweiss, pages 87–88, which clarifies this point.)

Exercise D

Rarely does the body of a theme consist solely of fact statements. Themes typically contain other kinds of statements as well—namely, *logic*, *opinion*, *definition*, and *example* statements. Hence, to enable you to concentrate entirely on fact statements, we have invented the special theme assignment that follows.

By consulting no fewer than three reference works such as biographies and encyclopedias, write a theme in which you explain why *one* of the compound fact statements below is entirely true, entirely false, or partly true and partly false.* (As was pointed out above, the mere assertion that a statement is true or false does not make the statement true or false. *Evidence* for the assertion is required.) Before doing this exercise, consult the *Model for Theme Analyzing a Compound Fact Statement* on page 84. Notice that the titles of your sources are to be cited in your theme. Notice, too, that this exercise deals with a *what* topic; that it calls for a thesis sentence; and that the thesis sentence observes the rules of relevance and parallelism. *Be sure to avoid borrowing the language of your sources, except in the most sparing way.*

1. Edgar Allan Poe, a poet, story writer, and critic who was born in Richmond, Virginia, in 1813, reviewed Henry Wadsworth Longfellow and wrote the tale "The Fall of the House of Usher."
2. Nathaniel Hawthorne was born in Jamestown, Virginia, on July 4, 1804, attended Bowdoin College, where he was a classmate of Henry Wadsworth Longfellow, and wrote the poem "Thanatopsis."
3. Henry David Thoreau lived at Walden Pond for fifteen years, after which he returned to his home in San Francisco, California, to write a book called *Walden*.
4. Alexander Hamilton, who was the legitimate son of a New York grocer, at age twenty-three became secretary of the treasury under President George Washington, under whom he had served as aide-de-camp during the Civil War.
5. James Fenimore Cooper, who was born in Philadelphia in 1819, wrote five novels called "The Leather-Stocking Tales," the names of which are *The Last of the Mohicans*, *The Pilot*, *The Deerslayer*, *The House of the Seven Gables*, and *The Spy*.
6. Thomas Jefferson, who married a widow, was the fifth president of the United States, founder of the University of Virginia, and lifelong friend of John Adams.
7. Daniel Webster, born in Connecticut, graduated from Dartmouth College, enjoyed a long career in Congress, and finally became vice-president of the United States.
8. John C. Calhoun, born in North Carolina in 1792 and educated at Yale, became secretary of war and then vice-president of the United States.
9. John Greenleaf Whittier, born in Mississippi in 1807, was very much in favor of slavery and wrote his poem "Ichabod" to attack Daniel Webster.

*If only because of the competition for source materials, your teacher may ask you to write a theme on a compound fact statement that he has originated.

10. Seven-foot-tall Abraham Lincoln was born in Virginia, reared in Kentucky, Indiana, and Illinois, and became president of the United States before he was killed by an assassin's knife.

11. Walt Whitman, born in 1809 on Long Island, New York, wrote a book of poems called *Figs of Grass*, which he published himself in 1855 before he married Margaret Fuller.

12. David Crockett, born in 1789 and reared on the Tennessee frontier, fought under Gen. Andrew Jackson, went to Harvard, eventually served two terms in Congress, and wrote an autobiography, the full title of which is *Davy Crockett: Frontiersman and Congressman*.

13. George Washington Cable, born in 1842 in New Orleans, fought in the Civil War on the side of the Union and eventually wrote a book called *Old Creole Days*, a collection of stories about Mexicans.

14. Samuel Langhorne Clemens, born in 1831 in Hannibal, Missouri, became a printer, a steamboat pilot, and author of *Life on the Mississippi* and *Death in the Afternoon*, besides marrying Edith Wharton and retiring finally in Alabama.

15. Henry James, born in 1840 in New York City, fought on the Confederate side in the Civil War and wrote such books as *Hawthorne*, *Johnny Get Your Gun*, and *The Wings of the Dove* before dying in Pennsylvania at age thirty-five.

16. Frank Norris, born in 1867 in California, never went abroad but studied instead at the University of California and at Yale, eventually writing such books as *McTeague*, *Forever Amber*, and *The Octopus*, for which he won the Nobel Prize for literature.

17. Theodore Dreiser, born in 1868 in Terre Haute, Indiana, of Irish parents, never left home but wrote instead a number of books, among them *Jennie Gerhardt*, *The American Tragedy*, and *Of Time and the River*.

18. Franklin Delano Roosevelt, born in 1883 in New York, was defeated in his race for the vice-presidency, contracted paralysis in his left arm, and finally managed to become President of the United States for five successive terms, initiating in the meantime his program called the New Deal.

19. William Cullen Bryant, born in 1792 in Massachusetts, went to New York when he was twenty-five to edit the *New York Evening Post* and to write such poems as "Thanatopsis," "The Raven," and "To a Waterfowl," matters which prevented him from writing editorials on behalf of the public.

20. James Russell Lowell, born in 1809 in Cambridge, Massachusetts, became a teacher of foreign languages at Harvard University (succeeding Edgar Allan Poe in that post), an editor of the *Nation* and the *Atlantic Monthly*, and minister to Spain and England, meantime marrying Maria Edgeworth and writing such books as *A Fable for Critics* and *The Biglow Papers*.

21. Ralph Waldo Emerson, born in 1809 in Boston, Massachusetts, of German immigrants, studied at Yale Divinity School and became a Unitarian minister, after which he wrote such books as *Nature* and delivered such discourses as "Self-Reliance" and "Compensation."

22. Herman Melville, born in New York City in 1828, became a sailor at age fifteen, lived in the South Sea islands for ten years, and married a native girl—experiences which provided him with the material for such books as *Typee*, *Moby-Dick*, and *Two Years before the Mast*.

23. John Dos Passos, born in 1894 in Chicago, attended Princeton University, from which he graduated in 1910, served as a lieutenant colonel in World War I, and wrote such novels as *Three Soldiers*, *Manhattan Transfer*, and the *Studs Lonigan* trilogy.
24. Carl Sandburg, born in 1878 in Chicago of immigrant parents, was a journalist in Milwaukee and Chicago who never married but who wrote such books of poems as *Smoke and Steel*, *The People*, *No*, and the ten-volume biography of Abraham Lincoln.
25. Edwin Arlington Robinson, the novelist, was born in 1865 in Head Tide, Maine, never married but became a steel worker before Theodore Roosevelt "discovered" him and gave him a government position so that he could continue to write such books as *The Children of the Night*, *Captain Craig*, and *The Congo and Other Poems*.

Model for Theme Analyzing a Compound Fact Sentence

(The compound fact statement assigned for the theme below was: Henry Wadsworth Longfellow, born in 1811 in Cambridge, Massachusetts, attended Bowdoin College, where he was a classmate of Nathaniel Hawthorne, and eventually became a professor and a poet whose bust was placed in the Poets' Corner of Westminster Abbey during his lifetime.)

Analysis of a Compound Fact Statement Relating to Henry Wadsworth Longfellow

Thesis sentence asserting that *S* (the compound fact statement) divides into two subsets (false and true fact statements) and that the first set contains three elements, the second, five.

The compound fact statement relating to Henry Wadsworth Longfellow contains three false and five true fact statements.

Subset of false fact statements

The statement that Longfellow was born in 1811 is false. According to the works I have consulted—namely, *Encyclopaedia Britannica*, *Dictionary of American Biography*, and Edward Wagenknecht's *Longfellow: A Full-Length Portrait*—he was born in 1807. The second false fact statement is that Longfellow was born in Cambridge, Massachusetts, when actually he was born in Portland, Maine. Cambridge was the town where he eventually lived when he became a professor at Harvard College (now University) in 1835. The third false fact statement is that his bust appeared in Westminster Abbey during his lifetime when, in reality, that honor was conferred upon him only after his death.

Subset of true fact statements

A true fact statement is that Longfellow attended Bowdoin College, according to my sources, an institution, which he entered in 1825 and from which he graduated. A second true fact statement is that Nathaniel Hawthorne was his classmate there—a meeting that ripened into a lifelong friendship between the two men. A third true fact statement is that Longfellow became a professor.

He taught modern languages at Bowdoin, his alma mater, from 1829 to 1835 and at Harvard from 1835 to 1854. Another true fact statement is that Longfellow was a poet. He became, in fact, one of the most popular poets America has known. Among his poems are "The Village Blacksmith," "Paul Revere's Ride," and "The Wreck of the Hesperus." The fifth and final true fact statement is that his bust was placed in the Poets' Corner of Westminster Abbey. He was the first American who received such a distinguished honor.

This theme, you will notice, expands a few lines into a well-organized, well-explained statement that bears such evidence and carries such conviction that no one is likely to argue with the writer. Keep in mind that **these are the objectives of paragraph development**.

Obviously, when a writer needs to adduce fact statements as evidence for his topic sentences (and fact statements are as serviceable for this purpose as they are indispensable), he should ascertain that his fact statements are indeed true. For if the reader detects a false fact statement, he is apt to question the writer's reliability and doubt the accuracy of other fact statements in the theme whose trueness he is unable to validate by his own knowledge. He might well ask, "How can I credit the writer's opinions if he can't even get his facts straight?" Such skepticism is hardly the response we ought to arouse in our reader if our object is, as it should be, to persuade him of the rightness of the positions we have presented in our topic sentences and, in consequence, of the value and soundness of our overall position represented by our thesis sentence.

Exercises E

The body of the specimen essay below consists almost entirely of fact statements. In reading it, answer these questions.

1. Do the fact statements strike you as true? Sufficient? Relevant?
2. Does the presentation of the fact statements persuade you that Poe really attempted to hoax his readers?
3. Does the writer treat his subject as a *what* or *why* topic? Explain.

A POE HOAX*

In writing "The Mystery of Marie Roget," Poe hit upon an extraordinary idea and was led to hoax his readers in the magazine and book versions of that tale.

Having introduced the detective story to the American public in "The Murders in the Rue Morgue," Poe felt challenged to better his performance. For the plot of his new tale he chose the actual unsolved murder in New York of a young woman named Mary Rogers; and with no more evidence before him than newspaper reports, for he was residing in Philadelphia at the time, he proceeded to solve the crime, alleging that the murder had been committed by a naval officer. Poe laid the story in Paris to make plausible the reappearance of his detective, C. Auguste Dupin, and called the tale, "The Mystery of Marie Roget." He submitted the some twenty-thousand-word story to at least three journals, one of which, Snowden's *Ladies' Companion*, chose to publish

*Adapted from the first author's review of John Walsh's book, *Poe the Detective: The Curious Circumstances Behind "The Mystery of Marie Roget"* (New Brunswick, N.J.: Rutgers University Press, 1968).

it in three installments. Only two installments of the tale had appeared (in November and December, 1842) when the police solved the crime, a solution totally incompatible with Poe's own. For no naval officer had been involved. Instead, Mary Rogers had been the victim of a criminal abortion.

With his reputation for ratiocinative power in jeopardy, Poe appears, with Snowden's complicity, to have held up the publication of the third and final installment until February 1843, while he apparently went to New York to learn the latest developments in the case and to square his "solution" as much as possible with the facts. These revisions account for the equivocations in the third installment and for Poe's warning readers that they should not make any detailed comparison of the fates of Marie Roget and Mary Rogers, despite the fact that earlier in the November installment he had invited readers to make just such a comparison.

When Poe reissued the narrative again in his *Tales* of 1845, he had made all the necessary adjustments by deleting statements inconsistent with the now ascertained facts and added the well-known footnotes. In the first footnote Poe says that the "mystery . . . had remained unsolved at the period when the present paper was written and published, yet that the confessions since obtained "long subsequent to the publication [of "Marie Roget"] confirmed, in full, not only the general conclusions, but absolutely *all* the chief hypothetical details by which that conclusion was attained."

This is the story that Mr. Walsh establishes for us in a narrative that is a profounder work of honest detection and shrewd conjecture than the tale whose background and text he researched and analyzed. His conclusion, that "Marie Roget" has enjoyed a "long and totally absurd existence as one of the supreme examples of Poe's analytical powers," is earned, validated as it is by the facts.

Logic Statements

Logic is the only *rational* process we have that enables us to pass connectedly from fact statement to fact statement; from fact statement to opinion statement; and from fact statement to opinion statement to opinion statement. See *Examples A* and *inference* in *Exercise A* below.

Examples A	1. From fact statement to fact statement	The wind sows the seed; the sun evaporates the sea; the wind blows the vapor to the field; the ice, on the other side of the planet, condenses rain on this; the rain feeds the plant; the plant feeds the animal.
	2. From fact statement to opinion statement	A man lost in the wilderness stumbled into a clearing where he saw a gallows. "Thank God!" he exclaimed, "I'm back in civilization!"
	3. From fact statement to opinion statement to opinion statement	Human beings cannot live without oxygen for more than a few minutes. The human-plant relationship is thus more important than human-human relationships. Therefore, ecology is a vastly more important study than psychology.

Intuition is another process, a very dramatic and significant one, of arriving at opinion. But it does so by skipping the rational process, or, as seems far more likely, by performing the rational process instantaneously. Physicists like Isaac Newton and Albert Einstein undeniably had brilliant intuitions, but their intuitions were in physics, not, say, in medicine or psychology; and their intuitions, moreover, related to problems in physics which they had been trying to de-puzzle for some time. At any rate, intuitions are not conscious but unconscious achievements that we cannot will to occur; and the results, in any case, have to be transposed to the rational process, as Newton and Einstein in fact did, if they are to be understood, shared, and possibly accepted by others.

Ignaz Philipp Semmelweiss (1818–65) was an Hungarian physician who in

1846 became Assistant in a Vienna maternity hospital. He found, as was common to such hospitals, puerperal fever raging in the wards, and doctors and nurses helpless to halt its spread or save its victims. When one of his colleagues became infected from a dissection wound and died, having shown symptoms identical to those of puerperal-fever victims, Semmelweiss had the brilliant intuition that doctors and interns were carrying infection from postmortem examinations back to their patients. At a time before Joseph Lister introduced the principle of antisepsis into surgery (which was to occur in the year of Semmelweiss's death), Semmelweiss urged that everyone assisting at childbirth first wash his hands in a solution of chlorinated lime.

Though this procedure dramatically reduced the incidence of childbirth fever in his maternity hospital, he was not reappointed in 1849 and was virtually hounded back to Hungary by personal and political persecution. Few of his own colleagues, let alone those elsewhere in Europe, were pleased to hear their hospitals called "murder holes" and themselves "medical Neros" who were committing "massacres."

Much as he brooded over the problem, Semmelweiss could not transpose his intuition to the rational process beyond the point of urging doctors to antisepticize themselves before performing their obstetrical duties. Long years of abrasive controversy, the knowledge that he had not discovered the cause of puerperal fever, and the guilt he suffered at knowing that he himself had unwittingly infected maternity patients, led to his breakdown, and he died in a mental institution from the same infection as was still killing many patients in lying-in hospitals. It remained for Pasteur, the founder of the science of bacteriology (see "How Louis Pasteur Discovered the Principle of Vaccination," pages 34–35), to accomplish the transposition that Semmelweiss was unable to accomplish; for Pasteur isolated the streptococcus and announced its discovery in 1879. In our terms Pasteur's achievement was that he converted Semmelweiss's opinion statement into a fact statement; or, to put it another way, he converted a *why* set into a *what* set, a process which characterizes the history of science.

The expressed results of logic are called logic statements, and they represent another kind of evidence by which the points of topic sentences are typically supported. And to support the points of our topic sentences by providing evidence for them is, to reemphasize, the objective of paragraph development.

Logic is not an end in itself; it is the means by which we pass from one statement to another, as is illustrated in *Examples A* above, something that should be kept in mind, notwithstanding that an entire chapter devoted to logic tends to create the opposite impression—that logic is an end in itself. In this chapter we shall be concerned with explaining how logic bridges the gap between fact statements and opinion statements. How this bridging can be done soundly will become still clearer in the next chapter devoted to opinion statements.

Exercise A:
Key Terms Used in
This Chapter

The terms below are most useful in discussing logic statements. Study them and their meanings and refer to them as often as necessary while reading this chapter.

assumption: anything taken for granted in the reasoning process and that serves as an unstated premise.

conclusion: the final stage in the reasoning process. When a conclusion derives *without fallacy* from true fact statements, it is a sound opinion. (See *inference*.)

consistency: logical connections among all phases of the reasoning process.

derive: to arrive at by reasoning; to deduce or infer.

derivable: that which can be inferred by reasoning.

equivocation: anything that balks the reasoning process. Equivocation occurs when a key expression has a variable meaning where a single fixed one is required. Equivocation also occurs when faulty or omitted punctuation allows for a double reading of a statement, or when the reasoning is circular. (See also *semantical argument*.)

fallacious: illogical reasoning in part or in whole.

fallacy: an error in reasoning.

follow: to occur or be evident as a logical consequence of what has been adduced.

hypothesis: a belief tentatively held for the purpose of testing (*testing* is the examining of relevant and sufficient evidence for or against a belief).

hypothesize: to assume something to be true which is not necessarily true.

hypothetical: said of a statement that may or may not be true.

inference: any statement, intermediate or final, in the reasoning process that is drawn from a premise or premises. When an inference represents the final stage in a reasoning process, and derives logically from true fact statements *without fallacy*, it is a sound opinion. (See *conclusion*.)

invalid: said of a reasoning process which is illogical in part or in whole.

non sequitur: a conclusion or inference illogically derived from, and therefore irrelevant to, its premise or premises.

posit: to set down as a premise.

premise: a statement which forms the basis, in whole or in part, for an inference.

semantical argument: a pseudo-argument stemming from failure to settle upon the meaning of a key term or terms. A semantical argument belongs to the class of equivocation in that it balks genuine discussion and often becomes a substitute for it.

sequitur: that which follows validly from a premise. If one is concerned with actual conditions, not hypothetical premises, the basis for the *sequitur* should be ascertained fact. If the basis for the *sequitur* is not ascertained fact, the *sequitur*, though validly derived, should be considered a *non sequitur* since it is irrelevant to actual conditions.

valid: said of a reasoning process which is logically executed.

Examples B:
Logic Statements

1. All human beings must die.
   X is a human being.
   Therefore, *X* must die.
2. All human beings must die.
   X must die.
   Therefore, *X* is a human being.

3. Anyone who "drinks" imbibes alcoholic beverages.
   Henry has wine, whiskey, and beer in his refrigerator.
   Therefore, Henry imbibes alcoholic beverages.
4. If *a* equals *b*, then *b* equals *a*.
5. If *x* equals *y*, then *y* does not equal *x*.
6. If sofa *a* weighs as much as sofa *b*, then sofa *b* weighs as much as sofa *a*.
7. If my house were made of cheese, it would be edible.
8. If Jane attends a Presbyterian church, she must be a Presbyterian.
9. If Tom is in college, he must be an *A* student.
10. If all human beings must die, then Richard must die.
11. Either the lamp in my house is illuminated or it is not.
12. Either the lamp in my house is black or it is white.
13. Either William married or did not marry.
14. Either William was married or divorced.

Three Forms of Logic Statement: Syllogism, "If . . . then," "Either . . . or"

Notice that typical logic statements such as appear in *Examples B* above take certain forms: (1) the syllogistic form; (2) the "if . . . then" form, even though the word *then* is sometimes implied rather than stated; and (3) the "either . . . or" form. Actually, all three forms are variations of a single basic form.

The Syllogism. Consider the least shortened of these three forms, the syllogism. It consists of a major premise, a minor premise, and a conclusion drawn from the two premises. Given its fullest form, one of the syllogisms in *Examples A* above would read:

Major premise: If all human beings must die,
Minor premise: And *if* X is a human being,
Conclusion: Then it follows that X must die.

Notice that the major and minor premises are clearly made hypothetical by the use of the *if's* (implied rather than stated in strict syllogistic form) and that, therefore, the premises do not necessarily belong to the set of fact statements in that (1) they do not claim to describe natural phenomena or historical events but only hypothesize such phenomena or events, and (2) they do not imply that the descriptions are necessarily true. To put it another way, logic per se is only concerned with the drawing of conclusions from premises.

The first premise of the syllogism is called *major* because it posits a set (the set of human beings in the example above) and a characteristic common to all elements belonging to that set (the characteristic of mortality). The second premise is called *minor* because X, relative to the first premise, is minor in that X is identified as only another element of the set of human beings. The *conclusion* drawn from the major premise ("If all human beings must die") and the minor premise ("And if X is a human being") is, therefore, unmistakable and irrefutable: "X must die."

But what if we now modify the minor premise, as was done with Example 2 in *Examples B* above, to read: "X must die"? Does X necessarily belong to the set of human beings simply because X shares a characteristic of human beings—

namely, their mortality? Or might *X* belong to another set of mortal things, such as the set of birds or the set of flowers? The answer, of course, is that we cannot tell to which set *X* belongs, but we can conclude that the inference "*X* belongs to the set of human beings" does not follow from the premises and is therefore invalid.

Exercise B

Consider Example 3 in *Examples B* above. Is the conclusion drawn from the premises valid or invalid, or is it conceivable that Henry might be a teetotaler in outright contradiction of the conclusion? Explain.

The *"if . . . then" form.* Consider the "if . . . then" form that logic statements commonly take, especially in themes and essays. The "if-clause" (as with major and minor premises of the syllogism) may refer to a real condition ("All human beings must die"), or to a possibly real condition ("If my house were made of cheese"), or to a pure abstraction ("If *a* equals *b*"). In all instances, however, the "if-clause" (as *if* suggests) is to be considered hypothetical in that it does not claim to be a fact statement. The "if-clause" only says in effect: "Grant me my premise and I shall draw a conclusion from it." Thus, with "if . . . then" forms of logic statements, we are not entitled to quarrel with the premise. We *are* entitled, however, to quarrel with the conclusion drawn from the premise when that conclusion does not follow from the premise (as we did earlier with the invalid conclusion drawn from the syllogism that appears as Example 2 in *Examples B*).

On the other hand, if we were urged to apply the conclusion formulated by the "then-clause" to a real situation, we would certainly be foolish not to question the factuality of the "if-clause" to assure ourselves that it is not merely a premise but a true fact statement. (See *sequitur* in *Exercise A* above.) To refer to one of our examples, you would want to know whether your house is made of cheese before you decide whether you wish to eat it.

Exercise C

Consider the "if . . . then" logic statements in *Examples B* above and explain why each of them is valid or invalid.

The *"either . . . or" form.* The "either . . . or" form is the most abbreviated of all forms of logic statements because only a conclusion is presented. For instance, in Examples 11 and 12 in *Examples B* above, the premise "If I had a lamp" is to be taken for granted, and only the validity of the conclusion is to be considered. Given this form of the logic statement, we are concerned only with what is called the **law of the occluded middle** (see the diagram below). The "either . . . or" form can be further condensed by omitting the "either," as in "My lamp is burning or it is not," or by omitting both the "either" and the "or," as in the declaration, "Strength lies not in defense but in attack."

Any statement that fails to occlude the middle tends to be misleading, as when Hitler declared in *Mein Kampf*, "Germany will be either a world power or will not be at all." Similarly, when someone asks, "Is the course good or bad?" we are apt to respond one way or the other, forgetting that some aspects of the course may be superior, while others may range from good to poor. When Patrick Henry concluded his famous address with the words, "Give me liberty or give me death," a colleague in the Virginia House of Burgesses is said to have rejoined, "But, Paddy, don't you have more reasonable alternatives?"

The Law of the Occluded Middle

Here the "middle" is occluded

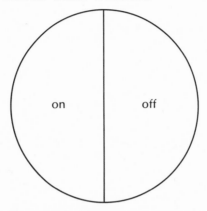

Here the "middle" is not occluded

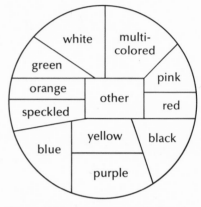

All possibilities in respect to the lamp's being illuminated or not are entirely exhausted by the "either . . . or" statement "Either my lamp is illuminated or it is not." Since no third possibility exists, the logic statement is said to be valid.

All possibilities in respect to the lamp's color are by no means exhausted by the "either . . . or" statement "Either my lamp is black or it is white." Since a third and even a hundred other possibilities still exist in respect to the lamp's color, the logic statement is said to be invalid.

Exercise D

Two of the four "either . . . or" statements in *Examples B* above occlude the middle and are therefore valid; two do not and are therefore invalid. Explain.

Simple and Compound Logic Statements

Simple logic statements, like *simple* fact statements, are two-valued in that they are either valid or invalid. (We do not say of logic statements that they are *true* or *false*, because the words *true* and *false* are reserved for the class of fact statements to designate accurate or inaccurate descriptions of natural phenomena and historical events; and logic statements, as we have said, only hypothesize such phenomena and events, and never claim to describe them accurately or inaccurately.) A logic statement is *valid* when its conclusion follows from its premise or premises; it is *invalid* when its conclusion does not follow from its premise or premises.

Compound logic statements can be treated as we treated compound fact statements (page 80), by anatomizing them into simple logic statements. Consider this compound logic statement: "If x, y, and z are equal, and b, c, and d are equal to x, then b, c, and d are equal to y and z." One simple logic statement derivable from this compound logic statement is: "If x and y are equal, and b is equal to x, then b is equal to y." What other simple logic statements can be derived from this example?

As was explained in another connection (page 81), to say that you *feel*, or *think*, or *believe* a logic statement to be valid or invalid does not convert it into a valid or invalid logic statement, any more than feeling, thinking, or believing you are Napoleon makes you Napoleon. Therefore, you should withhold such expressions. All you do when you add such expressions to logic statements is to adulterate the issue, for it is not your psychological state in regard to logic statements that is at issue, but logic statements themselves.

Since the premises of logic statements are hypothetical, and the conclusions are inferences drawn from those premises, we cannot prove logic statements as we prove fact statements—by referring to the phenomena or events being described. Instead, we prove or disprove logic statements by referring to the principles of logic, especially to the principle of consistency. "If x is equal to y, then y is unequal to x" is an example of a logic statement that violates the principle of consistency.

Exercise E

Identify the following two statements as either fact statements or logic statements: (1) If sofa a weighs as much as sofa b, then sofa b weighs as much as sofa a. (2) Sofa a weighs as much as sofa b.

As you no doubt have observed, to prove statement 1 in *Exercise E* above, you had only to refer to the principle of consistency. You had no need to consult reference works for the history of sofas, for instance, or bring in outsized scales. You were not even curious to know whether the sofas mentioned actually exist, for you were concerned with logic, not fact. Thus, you exerted yourself only mentally, not physically. As you have also observed, to prove statement 2 in *Exercise E*, you would have to bring in outsized scales and weigh each of the sofas in turn to compare their weights before you could determine whether the statement is true or false. Thus, **another characteristic of fact statements is that proof for them involves physical exertion**. Contrariwise, **another characteristic of logic statements is that they can be proved by mental exertion only**.

Exercises F

1. Construct three valid logic statements of your own, representing each of the three kinds of logic statements discussed above (the syllogism, the "if . . . then," and the "either . . . or" forms), and title your paper: Three Representative and Valid Logic Statements.
2. Construct three invalid logic statements of your own, representing each of the three forms discussed above, and title your paper: Three Representative and Invalid Logic Statements.

Common Kinds of Fallacies

The possibilities for making errors in reasoning are so many that an entire book would be required to treat the subject. We shall limit our examination, then, to only a few of the commoner errors. In examining the instances below, notice that **all fallacies, whatever their variety, belong to the class of non**

sequiturs. A *non sequitur* occurs when a conclusion does not follow from its premise or premises.

1. *Mistaken causal relation* (the fallacy of mistaking a concomitant relation for a cause-and-effect relation).

A principal expelled a boy from high school because he insisted on wearing his hair long. The boy's mother appealed to the school board to get her son readmitted, but the board upheld the principal's decision. "Your son," they said, "may return to school as soon as he wears his hair in a normal way." The outraged mother decided to take the case to court. In court, the mother's attorney produced last year's annual, which showed the boy with a crew cut. "You see," he said, "last year the boy had short hair and failed two subjects." At that, the attorney for the school board jumped to his feet and retorted, "But look at him this year. He has long hair and he is failing three subjects!"

(Point out the mistaken causal relation—the illogical connection between premise and conclusion—and demonstrate that, if we accept the logic of these lawyers, we would have to conclude that the services of a barber, not those of a teacher, would be sufficient to reduce the number of the boy's failures in high school.)

2. *Unwarranted generalization* (the fallacy of coming to a general conclusion on the basis of insufficient or improper evidence).

India has one of the highest birth rates in the world. Women who have trouble getting pregnant ought to go to India.

(Given the premise, why is the conclusion an unwarranted generalization?)

A nuclear scientist and former member of the Atomic Energy Commission estimated that 90 to 95 percent of our population could survive atomic bombings so long as they had "proper protection." In newspaper articles he described the "proper protection" that every householder could build for himself. Taking his own advice, the physicist constructed an inexpensive shelter of railroad ties and bags of soil in his backyard. Soon afterward the shelter was turned into a charred ruin by a brush fire.

(Had the scientist made an unwarranted generalization? Explain.)

3. *Oversimplification* (the fallacy of attributing a complex event to a single cause).

A famous gourmet devoted years to rating the quality of restaurants in the United States, and published his recommendations in a popular guidebook that became virtually indispensable to other gourmets. When the question was put to him on a "talk show": "What do you think is the cause for divorce?" he immediately answered, "Bad cooking."

(Does the conclusion "divorce" derive from the alleged cause "bad cooking," or is the gourmet's judgment an oversimplification?)

A psychiatrist alleged that comic books were bad for children. The evidence he provided was that he had been treating emotionally disturbed children for years and had discovered that they all had one thing in common: they all read comic books.

(Is the psychiatrist's evidence sufficient to explain emotional disturbance in children? Are all children who read comic books emotionally disturbed? Might the psychiatrist's "sample" be unrepresentative? (See Fallacy 6 below.) What factors other than comic books might be involved in the emotional disturbance of children?)

4. *Fallacious suggestion* (the fallacy of making a true statement misleading by suppressing crucial evidence).

A critic once said that Herman Melville was censorious of Ralph Waldo Emerson. Among the facts he cited to support his view was this: Melville had written in the margin of his Emerson book that Emerson insinuates "that had he lived in those days when the world was made, he might have offered some valuable suggestions."

(Among the suppressed facts are these: After Melville heard Emerson lecture, he wrote to a friend, "Say what they will, he's a great man!" and among Melville's other marginalia in the very Emerson book cited by the critic are such statements as: "Bully for Emerson! Good"; and "True and admirable! Bravo!" Given this additional evidence, do you consider the critic's conclusion to be valid?)

A national chain of food stores had millions of cans of yellow salmon in stock and could hardly sell a single one of them. Faced with serious financial loss, the chain employed the services of a Madison Avenue advertising agency. Within a week the cans were pyramided in all the chain's stores and bore the large sign:

YELLOW SALMON
GUARANTEED NOT TO TURN RED IN THE CAN

Within three days the entire stock of yellow salmon was sold.
(What words in the sign made a fallacious suggestion?)

5. *Statistical fallacy* (the fallacy of drawing invalid conclusions from a set of figures).

"This book must be twice as good as that one. After all, two people wrote this book and only one wrote that book."

(If the assumption is granted that "more is better," the conclusion is validly derived. Would you grant the assumption in this instance? Explain.)

In the space of one hundred and seventy-six years the Lower Mississippi has shortened itself two hundred and forty-two miles. That is an average of a trifle over one mile and a third per year. Therefore, any calm person, who is not blind or idiotic, can see that in the Old Oölitic Silurian Period, just a million years ago next November, the Lower Mississippi River was upwards of one million three hundred thousand miles long, and stuck out over the Gulf of Mexico like a fishing-rod. And by the same token any person can see that seven hundred and forty-two years from now the Lower Mississippi will be only a mile and three quarters long, and Cairo and New Orleans will have joined their streets together, and be plodding comfortably along under a single mayor and a mutual board of aldermen. There is something fascinating about science. One gets such wholesale returns of conjecture out of such a trifling investment of fact.—From Mark Twain's *Life on the Mississippi*.

(Twain is satirizing the abuse of *extrapolation*, a process that generally enables us to predict what will happen from what has happened. When not abused, extrapolation is legitimate, as in this instance: "Given the fact that

that we now have a college population of 10,000 and that our student enroll-
ment over the past decade has increased annually by 5 percent, it is probable
that we shall have a college population of 10,500 next year.)

6. *Unrepresentative sample* (the fallacy of biasing a survey, whether deliberately or inadvertently, so as to make what is unrepresentative appear representative).

A man was newly hired by a poll-taking agency to determine what, if any,
were the religious preferences of students on a given campus. He took his
stand one night outside the College Presbyterian Church and on another night
outside the Baptist Student Center. As the students came out, he put two
questions to them: (1) Do you have a religious faith? (2) To what church do
you belong, if any?

(What were the findings that this pollster reported to his agency? Why was
he discharged? Though the pollster's conclusion was validly derived from his
sample, was the sample a proper premise for his conclusion? What would you
do if you were given that pollster's assignment to ensure a representative
sample and thus representative results?)

Imagine the following situation: As head of a polling agency, you were com-
missioned in 1975 to make a study of magazine readership. To survey a large
and representative sample, you had your canvassers go from house to house at
random in a great variety of neighborhoods. When the results were tabulated,
you discovered a serious discrepancy: Far more people seemed to be reading
the *Atlantic* than *Penthouse*, despite the fact that certified publishers' figures
show that the *Atlantic* in 1975 was selling 329,359 copies to *Penthouse's*
3,809,364. You concluded that many of the people polled gave false answers
to your canvassers. You told them so in a meeting. One canvasser asked you,
"Why would they want to mislead us?" What answer did you give?

7. *False analogy* (the fallacy of citing an analogy that can lead to different or
   opposing conclusions).

If every neighborhood had its own fire station fully equipped with fire-
fighting apparatus, there would be no major fires in our country. By the same
logic, if every person had a gun, there would be no major crimes in our
country.

(Can an opposite conclusion be derived from this analogy?)

To dramatize his remarks on the evils of alcohol, a temperance preacher
was preparing to perform an experiment. "Watch carefully," he told his audience; "I am about to demonstrate what happens to a living creature caught in
the clutches of the fiery fiend." He took a worm between his fingers, held it
aloft so that the audience could watch it wriggle, then dropped it into a glass
of whiskey. In a few moments the worm ceased wriggling and died. "Now,"
the speaker addressed the audience triumphantly, "what does that prove to
you?"

(One answer made by a drunk in the audience was, "If you have worms,
drink whiskey.")

8. *Appeal to pity* (the fallacy of introducing an emotional factor unrelated to
   the logic of the situation)

Student to teacher: You oughtn't to fail me just because I didn't come to class or turn in my assignments. After all, I work forty hours a week to support my invalid mother and can't come to class, let alone do my assignments.

(The teacher, hearing this appeal, may feel pity for the student, but the conclusion "You oughtn't to fail me" is a *non sequitur* because it does not derive from the premise "I work forty hours a week to support an invalid mother." The premise, in short, is irrelevant to standards for passing.

A young man, about to be sentenced by a judge for murdering his parents, pleaded for clemency on the grounds that he was an orphan.

(If you were the judge, would you make the sentence lenient because of this appeal to pity? Explain.)

9. *Argumentum ad hominem* (the fallacy of *argument toward the man* rather than *toward the argument*: an attempt to discredit or recommend an argument by discrediting or recommending the person advancing the argument).

According to an often told but true story, the following statement was used by a politician to defeat his opponent in an election: "Are you aware that my opponent is known all over Washington as a shameless extrovert? Not only that, but this man is reliably reported to have practiced nepotism with his sister-in-law, and he has a sister who was once a thespian in wicked New York. He matriculated with co-eds at the University, and it is an established fact that before his marriage, he habitually practiced celibacy."

(Explain why this statement, though rather laudatory on the whole, succeeded in defeating the politician's opponent by *ad hominem* methods.)

10. *Appeal to authority* (the fallacy of attempting to prove a theoretical point by showing that others—so-called experts—happen to agree with you).

The following two statements were made during the course of a student debate:

"There is no question but that a great many of us in the United States would survive an atomic attack, provided, of course, we had sufficient bomb shelters. Dr. X, the Nobel Prize winner and a father of the hydrogen bomb, has stated that before the Senate Arms Committee."

"The truth is that few of us would survive an atomic attack, whatever protection we took against it. Dr. Y, the Nobel Prize winner and a father of the atomic bomb, has told us that quite convincingly in his celebrated book on nuclear warfare."

(The issue being theoretical, the testimony of one expert can be easily canceled out by the testimony of a second expert.)

"Professor Z, the world-renowned authority on China and the author of many articles and books about the Far East, agrees with me that we must not have a woman president in the foreseeable future. Women, he explains, are simply too gentle to cope with the harsh realities of international affairs."

(Is Professor Z's testimony of any relevance in this connection? Explain.)

Before leaving the subject of fallacies, we should touch upon another kind of common difficulty called *equivocation*. **Equivocation designates anything that balks the reasoning process.** The reasoning process can be balked when a key expression has a variable meaning where a single fixed one is required; or when faulty or omitted punctuation allows for a double reading of a statement; or when the argument is circular and makes discussion fruitless.

Exercises H:
Equivocation

1. "He is mad at his boss and anyone who is mad ought to be put in a mad-house."
   (In what two senses is the word *mad* used here? Can the argument progress fruitfully, or must it stop until the two meanings of *mad* are distinguished? Explain.)

2. When Richard Brinsley Sheridan, the playwright, was a member of the House of Commons, he called a fellow member a liar. Asked to apologize for his outburst, he said: "Mr. Speaker I said the honorable member was a liar it is true and I am sorry for it and the honorable member may place the punctuation marks where he pleases." (Punctuate Sheridan's statement so that it is really an apology. Now re-punctuate the sentence so as to confirm Sheridan's original charge. Was it Sheridan's purpose to advance or balk the argument? Explain.)

3. Among a state's statutes appeared this sentence: "No person may sleep in any hotel, dining room, rest room, or kitchen."
   (Why did hotel keepers in the state demand an immediate revision of this statute? Identify the faulty punctuation that balked an obvious piece of legislation.)

4. *Situation*: Mr. Jones has gone to a bank to establish his credit.
     Banker: Who will vouch for you, Mr. Jones?
      Jones: My friend Mr. Smith will vouch for me.
     Banker: Who will vouch for your friend Mr. Smith?
      Jones: Why, I would be happy to vouch for him.
   (Is the banker or Jones engaging in circular reasoning?)

5. Yossarian came to Doc Daneeka one mission later and pleaded again . . . to be grounded. . . .
     "You're wasting your time," Doc Daneeka was forced to tell him.
     "Can't you ground someone who's crazy?"
     "Oh, sure. I have to. There's a rule saying I have to ground anyone who's crazy."
     "Then why don't you ground me? I'm crazy. . . . Ask any of the others. They'll tell you how crazy I am."
     "They're crazy."
     "Then why don't you ground them?"
     "Why don't they ask me to ground them?"
     "Because they're crazy, that's why."
     "Of course they're crazy," Doc Daneeka replied. "I just told you they're crazy, didn't I? And you can't let crazy people decide whether you're crazy or not, can you?"
     Yossarian looked at him soberly and tried another approach. "Is Orr crazy?"
     "He sure is," Doc Daneeka said.
     "Can you ground him?"
     "I sure can. But first he has to ask me to. That's part of the rule."
     "Then why doesn't he ask you to?"

"Because he's crazy," Doc Daneeka said. "He has to be crazy to keep flying combat missions after all the close calls he's had. Sure, I can ground Orr. But first he has to ask me to."

"That's all he has to do to be grounded?"

"That's all. Let him ask me."

"And then you can ground him?" Yossarian asked.

"No. Then I can't ground him."

"You mean there's a catch?"

"Sure there's a catch," Doc Daneeka replied. "Catch-22. Anyone who wants to get out of combat duty isn't really crazy."

There was only one catch and that was Catch-22, which specified that a concern for one's own safety in the face of dangers that were real and immediate was the process of a rational mind. Orr was crazy and could be grounded. All he had to do was ask; and as soon as he did, he would no longer be crazy and would have to fly more missions. Orr would be crazy to fly more missions and sane if he didn't, but if he was sane he had to fly them. If he flew them he was crazy and didn't have to; but if he didn't want to he was sane and had to.—From *Catch-22* by Joseph Heller.
(Can "catch-22" lead to anything but circular reasoning?)

A final point that needs mentioning involves a principle of procedure summed up by the phrase "He who asserts must prove." As in a court of law, the burden of proof rests upon the person who asserts the proposition.

Exercises I:
"He Who Asserts Must
Prove"

1. "I'm sure there's some form of life on Neptune."
   "Can you prove it?"
   "No, but can you prove there isn't?"
2. One man is telling another that a bull had chased him up a tree. "Sure enough, it was just as I had dreaded; he started in to climb the tree—"
   "What, the bull?"
   "Of course—who else?"
   "But a bull can't climb a tree."
   "He can't, can't he? Since you know so much about it, did you ever see a bull try?"—From *Roughing It* by Mark Twain.

   (Who in these two instances must bear the burden of proof, according to the rule "He who asserts must prove"?)

10 **Opinion** Statements

To distinguish the set of opinion statements from other sets with which it might be confused, read the terms and their definitions in *Exercise A* below and refer to them whenever necessary while reading this chapter.

**Exercise A:
Key Terms Used in
This Chapter**

conviction: an opinion which one accepts unquestioningly and, when possible, may act upon. (The value of a hospital for sick people, conscientious objection to a war, Hitler's belief in Nordic superiority, John Wilkes Booth's idea that Lincoln had to be killed, are examples.)

hypothesis: a belief tentatively held for the purpose of testing (*testing* is the examining of relevant evidence for or against the belief). If the evidence, systematically and impartially examined and evaluated, vindicates the hypothesis the hypothesis becomes a *theory* (see below). If the evidence does not vindicate the hypothesis, the hypothesis is abandoned as untenable. (For example, what we now call the theory of evolution began as an hypothesis, and Charles Darwin spent thirty years examining evidence to test it, drawing upon the findings of paleontology, embryology, comparative anatomy, and experimental breeding, besides studying the geographical distribution of species.)

inference: any statement, intermediate or final in the reasoning process, that is drawn from a premise or premises. When the inference represents the final stage in the reasoning process, and derives logically (without fallacy) from true fact statements, it is a sound opinion.

law: a theory that has such a sufficient body of evidence that it is considered as one of nature's laws (such as Isaac Newton's laws of motion).

opinion: the class of inferences and conclusions. When an opinion derives logically (without fallacy) from true, relevant, and sufficient fact statements, it is a sound opinion. When an opinion derives illogically (with fallacy) from true fact statements, the opinion is unsound. When an opinion derives logically from untrue fact statements, the opinion is unsound.

theory: an hypothesis for which there is a considerable body of evidence but not sufficient to make it a law (as with Darwin's theory of evolution).

Opinion Statements Classified

Opinion statements can be classified according to the three positions they occupy in themes. When represented by *S* (the set to be supported in the body of the composition), the opinion statement occupies the *first major position*. When represented by *1 . . . n* (the reasons of *S*), opinion statements become topic sentences that explicitly (if stated) or implicitly (if unstated) govern each of the paragraphs. These opinion statements occupy the *second major position*.

The opinion statements of others, our own, or of both, that serve as evidence for the topic sentence occupy the *third major position*. The opinions of others are sometimes cited as evidence to bolster our own evidence, and such opinions have to be authoritative. The nature of authoritativeness varies from subject to subject. For instance, "Present student attitudes toward living in a dormitory" would call for the citation of student opinion, but the subject "The case for and against capital punishment" would call for the citation of relevant professional opinion—e.g., the opinions of criminologists, lawyers, sociologists, and psychologists. The opinion of such professionals, it should be noticed, would not be authoritative on the subject "Present student attitudes toward living in a dormitory," just as, on the whole, the opinions of students would not be authoritative on the subject "The case for and against capital punishment."

The opinions of others cited in our paragraphs may be quoted directly, or indirectly by paraphrase, but the source of these opinions should always be acknowledged (see footnote to page 29). Whether or not to cite the opinions of others is optional; the choice will be determined by the nature of the subject and the judgment of the writer.

Cited Opinions as Fact Statements

As was pointed out in the footnotes to pages 4 and 21, the opinions of others that we cite in our paragraphs are to be considered as fact statements. To cite our previous examples, it is a true fact statement that, according to the polls, more people had the opinion that Richard Nixon would be a better president than George McGovern. It is also a true fact statement that some people still have the opinion that no man walked on the moon—that the feat was only a television stunt or hoax. Even though this opinion is held in disregard of the facts, it nevertheless remains a fact that some people believe that the moon walks were television stunts or hoaxes.

The Multivalued Nature of Opinion Statements

Opinion statements serving as thesis sentences typically have reference to the social scene and claim that certain attitudes or certain courses of action ought or ought not to be taken.

An opinion statement is to the social scene what an hypothesis is to science —namely, a belief that needs to be tested and either abandoned as untenable or elevated, to the degree possible, to the status of a theory. But there are obviously significant differences between an opinion statement and an hypothesis. One need not rally others to a belief in an hypothesis, unless, of course, a testing of the hypothesis requires such large sums of money and such great numbers of experimenters that grants have to be sought. Instead, the researcher experiments under controlled conditions and proves or disproves his hypothesis. If he proves his hypothesis, he publishes his findings and anyone, given professional competence and access to pertinent apparatus, can duplicate his experiment and verify his conclusions. This is done, for example, in physics and chemistry classes, where students typically re-perform the classic experiments.

We cannot, however, take our opinion statement regarding the social scene to the laboratory, so to speak, and prove or disprove it as a scientist might. First of all, if we were freely to experiment with every opinion advanced, our own and others', we would be in the absurd position, for instance, of allowing and not allowing Mainland China into the United Nations at one and the same time. Secondly, too frequent testing of even nonconflicting opinions would make society too unstable and the course of our lives, therefore, unpredictable. Thus, if we want to have our opinions tested, we (and those who believe as we do) must first convince others that a given social experiment (whether on a small or large scale) is worth performing, despite the cost and upheaval involved, in that it promises to improve the existing situation.

To take an historical case: The opinion statement that we ought to conserve human resources by establishing a federal old-age insurance plan and a federal-state unemployment system, as well as a federal-state plan of supporting unemployable persons and rehabilitating the handicapped, was once considered workable by some people and unworkable by others. The debate was hotly waged before and since the passing of the Social Security Act of 1935. But now that there has been sufficient testing of the opinion statement, all of us are convinced that the scheme is workable, even though some may still argue that it is not desirable. The scheme, in fact, has proved so workable and, to many, so desirable that the counterproposal—that we ought to revoke the Social Security Act—seems unworkable and undesirable.

We have learned that a simple fact statement is two-valued because it is demonstrably true or false. We have also learned that a simple logic statement is two-valued because it is demonstrably valid or invalid. Thus, **fact statements and logic statements are not controversial**. To be sure, people will argue about fact and logic statements, but such arguments are pseudo-arguments because research on the one hand and mental exertion on the other makes it possible to settle the "argument" one way or the other. But opinion statements are markedly different from fact and logic statements in that they are not two-valued, but *multivalued*. Consider the *multiple values* exhibited in the opinions below that were expressed in the United States about China in the post-Korean-War period. The opinion statements, it will be noticed, do not fall neatly into two classes, but into many classes and subclasses, a point that the summaries below can only suggest.

Background Information concerning Chinese-American Relationships

China, a vast country, is the heart of Asia. China and the United States had a history of friendship; they were allies, for instance, in the Pacific campaigns of World War II. China, in the meantime, became communistic and sought to extend its power into South Korea, Taiwan, Vietnam, the Indian subcontinent, and the Japanese and Philippine archipelagoes. The United States sought to contain the expansion of Chinese power by refusing to recognize the government led by Premier Chou En-lai, recognizing, instead, the government led by Chiang Kai-shek on Taiwan; by opposing China's admission into the United Nations; and by fighting wars in Korea and Vietnam. China, for its part, considered the United States to be guilty of extending its spheres of influence; of obstructing China's rightful purposes; of exploiting the poor peoples of the world, at home and abroad; and of threatening atomic war.

American Opinions about China in the Post-Korean-War Period

1. The United States has adopted strictly defensive measures against China in an effort to contain her, as witness the wars in Korea and Vietnam. This is fair and as it should be.
2. The objective of the United States should be more farsighted, more courageous. Communism, not only in China but in Russia, must be destroyed as a political force. The best way to accomplish this is to overthrow the Chinese government first, then the Russian government.
3. The only way to overthrow the Chinese government would be to carry the war into China itself. But China is too vast a country to be effectively occupied by any military force or any combination of military forces. The sheer numbers of Chinese would make subjection of them impossible.
4. The success of the United States in the "cold" war with China depends to a great extent upon our relations with our allies and the uncommitted nations. Any action that we might take independently of them would probably result in our estranging them. To contain China, which seems our only hope in the circumstances, we need to strengthen our relations with our allies and seek to make new allies of the neutralist nations. The cold war with China must be reinforced, therefore, with bigger foreign-aid programs, with enlarged Peace Corps missions, and with stronger pledges of military support.
5. China now has the atomic bomb. If the United States does not take direct

action, China will soon find the means to destroy the United States. It seems only good sense to strike first with our atomic bombs. After all, the United States forced Japan to surrender by dropping atomic bombs on Hiroshima and Nagasaki in World War II.

6. The United States cannot take responsibility for starting World War III. Aside from the enormity of such an act, our use of atomic bombs would alienate our allies, antagonize the uncommitted nations, and would no doubt consolidate the Communist bloc, which is presently split. All this is assuming that the world would survive an atomic war.

7. There is certainly no immediate or total solution of the Chinese problem. The best we can hope to do is to solve one small part of the problem at a time. It is not inconceivable that time may be on our side. There could be a change in Chinese policy, and official negotiation might be renewed. Once China shows a readiness to settle matters peaceably, the United States should give its official recognition, as France has done, and invite China to be a member of the United Nations.

"Values" as Unstated Premises in Opinion Statements

What makes opinion statements controversial, multivalued, and very difficult to settle is that they contain unstated premises relating to "values" or a "value system"; and it is these very unstated and often unquestioned premises that subliminally shape the opinion. "Values" have to do with what is moral and immoral, aesthetic and unaesthetic, pleasurable and painful, wise and unwise, and these terms do not occlude the middle (see page 92) because there is a wide range between any of these pairs. Present statutes, for instance, hold petit larceny to be less immoral than grand larceny, and grand larceny to be less immoral than murder. Likewise, similar moral values are built into our present tax laws that encourage, among other things, marriage, not divorce, and childbearing, not childlessness.

Values obviously vary from person to person, sometimes only in degree, sometimes in kind. Lincoln, to illustrate the point, interrupted a would-be client by saying: "Yes, we can doubtless gain your case for you; we can set a whole neighborhood at loggerheads; we can distress a widowed mother and her six fatherless children and thereby get for you six hundred dollars to which you seem to have a legal claim, but which rightfully belongs, it appears to me, as much to the woman and her children as it does to you. But you must remember that some things legally right are not morally right. We shall not take your case, but will give you a little advice for which we will charge you nothing. You seem to be an energetic man; we would advise you to try your hand at making six hundred dollars in some other way."

A value system, as the expression suggests, is a set of values in more or less hierarchical order, like that represented by the statutes cited. In Lincoln's value system moral rights generally had a higher priority than legal rights.

Values and value systems, as we said, have also to do with aesthetics. Some people prefer "classical" to "popular" music, Rembrandt's paintings to pop posters, Gothic cathedrals to geodesic domes, or vice versa. Likewise with pleasure and pain: some people consider creative work in all its remarkable variety pleasurable, whereas others consider it painful.

Values are also involved in judgments of what is wise and unwise—terms usually applied to courses of action. The American Transcendentalists, for example, divided into communitarians and individualists, not so much because their values differed as because their courses of action did. One group led by George Ripley believed that individual regeneration would occur as a consequence of reforming the social system; whereas another group, of whom Ralph Waldo Emerson was the chief spokesman, believed that reform of the social system would occur only as a consequence of individual regeneration.

The point is that everyone has values by which he lives. When Christ said, "It is written, 'Man shall not live by bread alone,' but by every word that proceedeth out of the mouth of God," he was saying that man must live by the highest values, those associated with God. Emerson identified some of those values as friendship, love, truth, and harmony. A novelist, to emphasize the *value* of values, wrote, "If a person has nothing to die for, he has nothing to live for." And Plato suggested by his Triad, "The Good, the True, and the Beautiful," that the moral, the wise, and the aesthetic are not separable but are three aspects of the same thing, devotion to which produces the highest happiness in a person.

Another thing that makes opinion statements very difficult to settle is that they tend to arouse emotion, an emotionalism that warps the reasoning process. Such emotions are aroused because a great many people feel varying degrees of threat when they hear or read opinions contradictory or even at variance with their own. No doubt the fact statement "The United States has a welfare system," and the logic statement "If all human beings must die, I must die," have the power to arouse emotion in someone; but the opinion statement "We should exterminate everyone presently on welfare" is liable to arouse very powerful emotions in everyone and not all of the same degree or kind.

But emotionalism, insofar as it precipitates the process of reason and research, is as necessary as it is valuable. One would scarcely be concerned with arriving at any opinion unless he were emotionally involved in the problem in the first place, something to which scientists, though notable for their detachment, are as susceptible as anyone else. But emotionalism too often enters into the process of reason and research and thereby tends to prejudice the results of that process, again a condition to which scientists are far from immune. Emotionalism, in other words, can easily short-circuit an impartial examination of the evidence upon which opinion statements are or, ideally, ought to be predicated. Far too often it is not truth we are after but a defense of our prejudgments, the judgments that, based on our values, we had before we examined the evidence. What further complicates the problem is that reason and rationalization are twin processes, distinguishable more by their intention than by their mode of operation—whether, in other words, we are seeking the truth in a given instance or only a quasi-rational support for our prejudices. In varying degrees, such emotionalism or prejudice is common to all human beings, for reasons which Aldous Huxley clarifies by exaggeration in *Brave New World*. But if the educated person is to be distinguished by any one sign and if he is entitled to consider himself truly enlightened, it is that he is prepared to consider the available evidence concerning an opinion statement and is ready to accept, reject, or modify that opinion statement upon the evidence, even at the cost of his own prejudgments and values.

Exercises B

1. Opinion statements occupy three positions in themes. Identify these positions.
2. We said that *cited opinions* are fact statements. Explain.
3. What is meant by *multivalued*, *values*, and *value system*?
4. Distinguish between the processes we have designated as *reason* and *rationalization*.
5. In regard to matters of opinion, why is emotionalism good? Bad?
6. Write a theme entitled: Two Opinions I Feel Very Strongly About. (a) In your thesis sentence clearly specify your two opinions; (b) in subsequent paragraphs *do not* expound your opinions, but simply explain whether you would change your mind about one or both of them *if you encountered evidence unquestionably contrary to them*, and why you would or would not be willing to change your mind. Do not try to short-circuit this exercise by arguing that it is impossible to imagine evidence contrary to your two opinions. Such an argument only suggests that one has very little imagination.

Exercises C

Discuss in class each of the opinion statements below. Which of them do you accept? Oppose? Which would you find acceptable if something in the opinion statement were modified? Would you want to consider the implications of each of those opinion statements for our society and for the world at large and qualify your position accordingly?

1. The death penalty should be made mandatory in the United States for rape, kidnapping, and murder.
2. Polygamy in the United States should be as legal as monogamy.
3. To demonstrate its desire for world peace, the United States should withdraw its troops from all foreign countries, dismantle all its missile bases, and send food, not arms, abroad.
4. The heroin traffic should be legalized in the United States so that heroin addicts will not have to commit crimes to support their habit and so that crime syndicates will not be able to profit from the traffic.
5. Financially troubled cities should not be aided by the federal government.
6. National Health Insurance for everyone should not be tolerated in the United States.
7. Doctors should have the legal right to practice euthanasia.
8. Abortions should be illegal in the entire United States.
9. The sale of cigarettes should be made illegal in the United States because most doctors believe that cigarette smoking contributes to lung cancer and heart attacks.
10. Misfits should be sterilized.

As you have no doubt learned from your classroom discussion, such statements as those that appear in *Exercises C* above cannot be settled to everyone's satisfaction in the way we can settle fact and logic statements. For that reason there are multitudes who disagree, often violently, about opinion statements compared to those who disagree about fact and logic statements. In fact, we tend to call those who dispute true fact statements uneducated and those who dispute valid logic statements obtuse; but, paradoxically, we also say that everyone has a right to his opinion. Yet that too is an opinion statement and, as such, is open to discussion. For all we really mean by the statement "Everyone has a right to his opinion" is that everyone has, or ought to have, a constitutional right to express his opinion freely and without fear of reprisal—in short, the right of free speech. We surely do not mean that everyone's opinion is as sound as everyone else's. The opinion statement "Herman Melville was an admirer of Emerson" is sounder than the opinion statement "Herman Melville was a literary enemy of Emerson" for the reasons that were suggested on page 95. And surely a medical doctor, once he has made clinical studies of his patient (when, in other words, he has arrived at true fact statements), is better equipped to make sounder opinion statements about his patient's condition than, say, the ward mate of the patient.

These examples demonstrate what makes one opinion sounder and therefore more persuasive than another. **An opinion statement becomes increasingly sounder (1) as it supports itself by a greater number of relevant facts and (2) as it partakes more of the nature of a valid inference drawn from those facts.**

**Exercises D:
Judging the Soundness
of Opinion Statements**

Consider the three examples below and explain which opinion is sounder in each instance.

1. *Layman*: You're nervous; that's your trouble. You drink too much coffee and smoke too many cigarettes. I know; I had the same trouble myself last year.
   Doctor: According to the gastrointestinal series I ran on you, you have an ulcer which really ought to be surgically removed.

2. *Patient* (buttonholing a doctor on the street): Doctor, I haven't time to go to your office, but I'm sure you can tell me what my trouble is. (Patient proceeds to cite his symptoms.)
   Doctor: It sounds like an ulcer, but come to my office when you have time.
   Doctor: (having made clinical tests of his patient): Your trouble is that you have a duodenal ulcer.

3. *Two reports on clergymen's income that appeared in 1965*
   a. A survey of 11,000 parish clergymen in the United States, conducted by the National Council of Churches, shows that the median clergyman's salary is $5,158—a figure that falls from $1,000 to $1,900 below the salaries of other workers of comparable training and skill. Yet the median income for clergymen fails to tell the whole story. The provision that is made for their automobile expenses, utilities, and housing, not to mention business costs, is so inadequate that only 4 percent of them actually draw even this income. Most of them, in effect, are forced to subsidize their ministries out of their own salaries. So poor is the salary of the average American clergyman that 15 percent of them find it necessary to "moonlight" (to drive school buses, for instance, or work extra hours as

clerks) an average of 9.4 hours per week; and 4 percent moonlight as many as 20 or more hours per week. When we also consider that one-fifth of the clergymen have wives who work, half of them full-time, we can realize in what dire financial straits our clergymen are foundering.

b. On the whole, clergymen in the United States seem to be very well paid, not to mention the fact that they receive fees, free goods, free services, and discounts that supplement their incomes. I know two ministers who have very elegant churches, quite wealthy congregations, and who drive Lincoln Continentals. Even those ministers who do not have such fine churches and such fine congregations earn, I am sure, far more than others with similar training and responsibilities.

Earlier we noticed that opinion statements contain implied and often unquestioned values. What is the "value" or implied standard of judgment of the two speakers in each of the examples below that causes them to come to conflicting conclusions?

1. *First speaker*: This is an easy course.
   Second speaker: Easy! It's tough!
2. *First speaker*: This college has a lovely campus.
   Second speaker: Lovely! You should see Southern Illinois's campus!

Once we have detected the implied standards (the unstated premises) in the reactions given above, we recognize that there are no legitimate grounds for argument. Explain.

As we said earlier, the bridge between fact statements and opinion statements is logic. A sound opinion statement is in the nature of an inference. If the fact statements do not satisfy the conditions of accuracy, relevance, and sufficiency, all logic statements drawn from those facts, however validly, are suspect and the opinion remains doubtful. If the fact statements satisfy the three specified conditions, but the logic statements drawn from them are invalidly inferred, the opinion statement still remains doubtful. **In short, an opinion statement is sound when and only when it is reached by means of true, relevant, and sufficient fact statements and when valid inferences are drawn from those fact statements.**

Exercises E

1. Of the three kinds of statements we have thus far discussed—namely, fact, logic, and opinion statements—which would tend to predominate in ordinary conversation? At the meeting of a learned society? Explain.
2. Who is likelier to have more numerous and more positive opinions, and who at the same time is likelier to express those opinions with greater assurance—one who has done little study of a given subject or one who has devoted a career to the subject? In this connection consider the professor of cybernetics (cybernetics is the study relating to computers and computer theory). During a TV interview he was asked, "Do you believe that computers think?" His reply was, "If you had asked me that question ten years ago, I would have answered immediately, 'They certainly do not think.' Now I say I really don't know. Ten years from now I shall probably be inclined to say that computers think."
3. Below appear various kinds of statements. (a) Identify each of them as either

fact statement, logic statement, or opinion statement, and (b) determine whether the fact statements are true or false or partly true; whether the logic statements are valid or invalid; and whether the opinion statements are sound or unsound.

a. Jim earns higher grades on his themes than I.

b. If Jim earns higher grades on his themes than I, then Jim is superior to me.

c. Texas is located at the northernmost tip of the United States and is popularly known as the Lone Star State.

d. The most heavily populated state in the United States is New York.

e. The major problem of the college freshman is that of adjusting to a new kind of life in which he is expected to behave as an adult.

f. Love is the dominant emotion in every living person.

g. Shakespeare was either a playwright or he wasn't.

h. Shakespeare was either born in Africa or in Australia.

i. The late President Franklin D. Roosevelt, a victim of infantile paralysis, founded the National Foundation for Infantile Paralysis in 1939 in order to support scientific research into polio as well as to give aid to thousands of polio victims.

j. Birds are common; a whooping crane is a bird; therefore, whooping cranes are common.

k. All dogs are carnivorous; Labrador retrievers are dogs; therefore, Labrador retrievers are carnivorous.

l. Of course it wasn't my fault; I have never been in an automobile accident before.

m. Abraham Lincoln was president of the United States for three successive four-year periods.

n. The bed must be the most dangerous object in civilization, for most people die in it.

To enable you to apply what you have learned about fact and opinion statements (logic will be implicit throughout your paper), the following theme assignment has been devised, *the sole purpose of which is sound paragraph development*. For this reason you are given the topic, the title, the thesis sentence, and various clues to paragraph development. When you have read the instructions below, examine the model theme that appears on pages 111–12.

Theme assignment: to analyze certain fact and opinion statements made about a prominent American in one of the paragraphs below.*

Purpose: (1) to organize a theme with faultless rigor; (2) to distinguish between fact and opinion statements; and (3) to develop paragraphs to the point of conviction.

Directions: The theme should run from 400 to 500 words. Before you begin to write this theme, you have first to do a twofold process of classification, which can be easily accomplished if you follow this procedure: (1) classify the statements found in your assignment into fact statements and opinion statements (see *Clues for classification* below); (2) consult reference works as prescribed in *Sources* below; (3) on the basis of your research, further classify

*If only because of the competition for source materials, your teacher may ask you to write a theme on a paragraph he has originated.

the statements to sort out true fact statements from false ones and sound opinion statements from unsound ones.

In writing the theme explain (1) why certain fact statements are true, **paying particular attention to precise details** so that the skeletal facts are fleshed out; (2) why certain fact statements are false, supplying all the evidence you need for declaring them false; (3) why certain opinion statements are sound, adducing all necessary fact statements to support those opinions; and (4) why certain opinion statements are unsound, supplying all necessary fact statements for declaring them unsound.

Organization: Your theme should have this title: An Analysis of Certain Fact and Opinion Statements about *X* (*X* is the name of the person you have been assigned for this theme). The theme should have as its thesis sentence: There are certain fact and opinion statements made about *X*, some of which are sound and others unsound.

Each of the succeeding four paragraphs will have a topic sentence specifying the set being discussed. Thus, the second paragraph will read: One true fact statement made about X is. . . . This statement will be followed by a discussion devoted to proving that the fact statement is true. Another sentence in the same paragraph will read: A second true fact statement is. . . . This sentence will be followed by a discussion devoted to proving that the statement is true. This paragraph will continue to have such statements followed by such discussion until you have exhausted the elements in the set of true fact statements. A third paragraph will deal with false fact statements, a fourth with sound opinion statements, and a fifth with unsound opinion statements, in the manner described above. Should you have a statement or statements that cannot be ascertained to be sound or unsound in the light of reasonable research, you are to have an additional paragraph devoted to "unprovable" statements. The topic sentence of this paragraph might read: One fact statement that cannot be proved in the light of available evidence is . . . , followed by an explanation of why that is the case.

Sources: You should use at least three or more sources. Various encyclopedias, the *Dictionary of American Biography*, and biographies are especially recommended. Somewhere in the second paragraph of your theme (where you deal with true fact statements), you should cite the reference works you have consulted. For example, "U. S. Grant, according to *Collier's* and *Encyclopaedia Britannica*, attended West Point. . . ." Do not use footnotes or a bibliography. Subsequent references to your sources should be made gracefully, with such phrases as "in the sources mentioned," "in the works alluded to," "all sources agree," unless, of course, you have reason to cite a particular source again. You are, needless to say, to borrow the relevant information you find in your sources, but *you are not to borrow the language of your sources except in the most sparing way*.

Clues for classification: A sign of an opinion statement is usually a modifier, either an adjective or adverb. To say that Andrew Jackson was a *backwoodsman* is to express a fact statement, either true or false, but to say that Andrew Jackson was an *uncultured* backwoodsman is to combine an opinion statement (either sound or unsound) with a fact statement (see the model theme below). Similarly, it is a fact statement to say that George B. McClellan was a general in the Union Army, but is an opinion statement to say that General

McClellan handled his troops *badly*. Such opinion statements require true fact statements for proof or disproof of them.

Model Theme for an Analysis of Fact and Opinion Statements

(*The assignment*: Andrew Jackson was an uncultured backwoodsman who became a military hero. He was a weak president. He justified presidential appointments by the slogan "To the victor belong the spoils."

An Analysis of Certain Fact and Opinion Statements about Andrew Jackson

Thesis Statement

There are certain fact and opinion statements made about Andrew Jackson, some of which are sound and others unsound.

Set of true fact statements

One true fact statement is that Jackson was a backwoodsman, at least in the dictionary sense of one who "comes from the backwoods." According to *Encyclopaedia Britannica*, *Collier's*, and *Encyclopedia Americana*, he was born in the Waxhaw settlement near the borderline between North and South Carolina and was raised in that frontier region. A second true fact statement is that Jackson became a military hero. According to my sources, he was idolized for his military exploits after his army defeated the British in the battle of New Orleans on January 8, 1815. His record in that battle was especially spectacular, for though the British suffered two thousand casualties in killed, wounded, and captured, Jackson's army suffered only thirteen—seven killed and six wounded.

Set of false fact statements

One false fact statement is that Jackson justified presidential appointments by saying, "To the victor belong the spoils." The sources mentioned affirm that he definitely approved of the spoils system, but *Encyclopedia Americana* attributes the phrase to William Learned Marcy (1786–1857). While defending the political-patronage policies of Jackson in a speech to the Senate in 1832, Marcy declared, "We can see nothing wrong in the maxim that to the victors belong the spoils of the enemy."

Set of sound opinion statements

An opinion statement that is sound in that Jackson was uncultured. According to *Encyclopedia Americana*, Jackson received very little education, as he had small opportunity for formal study or any other form of culture. The fact is that he never learned even to write correct English. Although he was admitted to the bar in 1787 and later served as a judge in the Tennessee Supreme Court, it is generally believed that his knowledge of law was extremely limited. *Collier's* does not regard Jackson as cultured, and *Encyclopaedia Britannica* flatly calls him uneducated.

Set of unsound opinion statements

An opinion statement that is unsound is that Jackson was a weak president. According to *Encyclopedia Americana*, Jackson greatly enlarged the importance and influence of the presidential office and is, therefore, to be considered one of the strongest presidents to have held that office. He was among the first presidents to advocate rule by the people, and it was his idea that the president should interpret the will of the people himself and execute that will without interference from either Congress or the Supreme Court. *Collier's* adds that Jackson's influence was so great that it was a decisive factor in the election of Martin Van Buren, the Democratic candidate, in 1836.

Set of "unprovable"
statements

[Since the paragraph assigned contained no "unprovable" statement, this remains an empty or null set. If, however, despite conscientious research, you should not be able to ascertain whether a statement is sound or unsound, you would add this paragraph to your theme explaining why you found that statement "unprovable." See page 110 under *Organization*.]

Statements for Analysis

1. U. S. Grant, whose full name was Ulysses Simpson Grant, was a poor boy who was sent to West Point, where he proved to be a very weak student. As an officer, he was reprimanded for drunkenness and compelled to resign his commission. Although he was not a very good tactician, his tenacity won him many victories. His presidency was untouched by scandal.

2. Eugene V. Debs, who was of Russian descent, ran for president of the United States three times on the Socialist ticket. He was once a locomotive fireman and eventually organized the American Railway Union. The strike he led was for a bad cause, and it was only right that he was arrested for conspiracy to murder. It was also right that he was jailed for being a pacifist.

3. Thomas Paine was born in America in the sixteenth century. Benjamin Franklin was chiefly responsible for his coming to Philadelphia. Paine performed great services in the Revolutionary War, though he was wrong in clinging to his principles while he was in France and deserved to be imprisoned there.

4. Roger Williams was a lawyer who founded Providence, Rhode Island. He was expelled from Massachusetts Bay Colony because of certain bad views he held, and his expulsion was therefore deserved. He is credited with founding the first Baptist Church in the New World. He was among the first champions of democratic principles in America.

5. Ernest Hemingway was born in Sheboygan, Wisconsin, where he lived most of his life. He served in an American volunteer ambulance unit during World War I. After the war he worked for a newspaper. He lived an adventurous life and died bravely, but his books are trash.

6. Paul Revere was a great American patriot. He saved the city of Boston singlehandedly because of his midnight ride, which was one of the turning points of the Revolutionary War. His deed became the subject of a poem by Henry Wadsworth Longfellow. Once he had made his midnight ride, however, Revere no longer performed important services for his country.

7. William Faulkner, the Mississippi writer, finished college with an M.A. in English. Avoiding involvement in World War I, he worked as a postmaster and later as a journalist. Although he was unexperimental in his writing, most of his books have a deservedly high reputation.

8. William Lloyd Garrison was a most moderate abolitionist. Although jailed

for his abolitionist activities, he continued to speak against slavery and to publish his views in the newspaper the *Liberator*. He thought force should not be used to end slavery. He was widely admired by all abolitionists. After the Civil War ended, he lost interest in public affairs.

9. Patrick Henry, born in North Carolina, was a successful storekeeper and farmer. He was well known as a statesman and became famous for his perfectly logical speeches. Though he advocated that the colonies separate from England, he opposed the adoption of the Constitution of the United States.

10. David Crockett was an educated man, who was born on a mountaintop in Tennessee and killed a bear when he was only three years old. As a member of Congress, he displayed poor statesmanship. This great hunter was killed in the battle of the Alamo.

11. Theodore Roosevelt, the twenty-fifth president of the United States, was a member of the Democratic party all his life. He had a full political career. He secured the rights and territory for the construction of the Panama Canal. However, his record as president was, all in all, a poor one. The Teddy bear was named after him.

12. Abraham Lincoln, the seventeenth president of the United States, was born in Kentucky. He was a Democrat and his early career in politics was very successful. He opposed slavery, was twice elected president, and his life was abruptly ended by an assassin. His death passed almost without notice because of the Civil War.

13. Oliver Wendell Holmes, son of Oliver Wendell Holmes, the American writer, was educated at Harvard College. He did not fight in the Civil War, but became a lawyer instead. Though a member of the Supreme Court, he was never distinguished for legal learning, humor, judgment, or power of expression. He was known as a liberal interpreter of the Constitution.

14. Henry George, born in Boston in 1840, was an important social reformer and economist in his time. He opposed the development of the railroads and advocated a policy called the Single Tax. His many books, written to explain why widespread injustice and poverty could not be eliminated, are considered of very little value.

15. Thomas Jefferson, third president of the United States, had a very rich political career. He wrote the Declaration of Independence and the Constitution of the United States, founded the University of Virginia, and favored slavery and religious freedom. His views, taken all in all, were undemocratic.

Example Statements

A fourth kind of statement that typically appears in themes can be designated *example statements*. Example statements consist of a single illustration, a single fact statement, or a single detail; or of multiple illustrations, fact statements, or details. Example statements serve almost every conceivable purpose, so we shall classify them here according to their two major purposes—whether they are intended (1) to support an assertion or (2) to illustrate an idea. When examples are adduced to support an assertion, they constitute evidence for that assertion. When examples are adduced to illustrate an idea, they are orientative or explanatory.

As was suggested, example statements can also be subclassified by number —whether, in other words, they contain single or multiple examples. Example statements by purpose and number appear below. You should notice that, in addition to satisfying the two purposes specified above, example statements make the vague vivid by supplying concrete detail and convert dullness into forcefulness by introducing striking particularities and instances.

Multiple EXAMPLE Statements to Support an Assertion

Example statements constitute *evidence* only when they are adduced to support an assertion. In such instances *multiple* examples must be cited, not just a single one. It may be taken as a rule that the broader the assertion, the more numerous must be the examples cited. The two selections below demonstrate these points.

Assertion

The history of the present King of Great Britain is a history of repeated injuries and usurpations, all having in direct object the establishment of an absolute tyranny over these states.

Multiple examples to support the charge of "repeated injuries and usurpations" by "the present King of Great Britain"

To prove this, let facts be submitted to a candid world.—He has refused his assent to laws, the most wholesome and necessary for the public good.—He has forbidden his governors to pass laws of immediate and pressing importance, unless suspended in their operation till his assent should be obtained. . . . —He has refused to pass other laws for the accommodation of large districts of people, unless those people would relinquish the right of representation in the legislature, a right inestimable to them and formidable to tyrants only.—He has called together legislative bodies at places unusual, uncomfortable, and distant from the depository of their public records, for the sole purpose of fatiguing them into compliance with his measures.—He has dissolved representative houses repeatedly, for opposing with manly firmness his invasions on the rights of the people.—He has refused for a long time, after such dissolutions, to cause others to be elected; whereby the legislative powers, incapable of annihilation, have returned to the people at large for their exercise; the state remaining in the meantime exposed to all the dangers of invasion from without, and convulsions within.—He has endeavored to prevent the population of these states; for that purpose obstructing the laws for naturalization of foreigners; refusing to pass others to encourage their migrations hither, and raising the conditions of new appropriations of lands.—He has obstructed the administration of justice, by refusing his assent to laws for establishing judiciary powers.—He has made judges dependent on his will alone, for the tenure of their offices, and the amount and payment of their salaries.—He has erected a multitude of new offices, and sent hither swarms of officers to harass our people, and eat out their substance.—He has kept among us, in times of peace, standing armies without the consent of our legislatures.—He has affected to render the military independent of and superior to the civil power.—He has combined with others to subject us to a jurisdiction foreign to our constitution, and unacknowledged by our laws; giving his assent to their acts of pretended legislation:—For quartering large bodies of armed troops among us:—For protecting them, by a mock trial, from punishment for any murders which they should commit on the inhabitants of these states:—For cutting off our trade with all parts of the world:—For imposing taxes on us without our consent:—For depriving us in many cases of the benefits of trial by jury:—For transporting us beyond seas to be tried for pretended offences:—For abolishing the free system of English laws in a neighboring province, establishing therein an arbitrary government, and enlarging its boundaries so as to render it at once an example and fit instrument for introducing the same absolute rule into these colonies:—For taking away our charters, abolishing our most valuable laws, and altering fundamentally the forms of our governments:—For suspending our own legislatures, and declaring themselves invested with power to legislate for us in all cases whatsoever.—He has abdicated government here, by declaring us out of his protection and waging war against us:—He has plundered our seas, ravaged our coasts, burnt our towns, and destroyed the lives of our people.—He is at this time transporting large armies of foreign mercenaries to complete the works of death, desolation and tyranny, already begun with circumstances of cruelty and perfidy scarcely paralleled in the most barbarous ages, and totally unworthy the head of a civilized nation.—He has constrained our fellow citizens taken captive on the high seas to bear arms against their country, to become the executioners of their friends and brethren. . . . —From the Declaration of Independence

Assertion

Multiple examples involving contradictions between the religious spirit supposed to characterize a clergyman and the anti-

It is hard to understand how the religious spirit can exist aboard a warship.

How can it be expected that the religion of peace should flourish in an oaken castle of war? How can it be expected that the clergymen, whose pulpit is a forty-two-pounder, should convert sinners to a faith that enjoins them to turn the right cheek when the left is smitten? How is it to be expected that when, according to the . . . Articles of War, as they now stand unrepealed on the

religious conditions in which the chaplain finds himself aboard a man-of-war

Statute Book, "a bounty shall be paid" (to the officers and crew) "by the United States Government of $20 for each person on board any ship of an enemy which shall be sunk or destroyed by any United States ship"; and when, by a subsequent section . . . , it is provided, among other apportionings, that the chaplain shall receive "two twentieths" of this price paid for sinking and destroying ships full of human beings? How is it to be expected that a clergyman, thus provided for, should prove efficacious in enlarging upon the criminality of Judas, who, for thirty pieces of silver, betrayed his Master?—From *White-Jacket* by Herman Melville.

Multiple EXAMPLE Statements to Illustrate an Idea

In addition to providing evidence for assertions (pages 114–15), multiple example statements serve to illustrate an idea. The two selections below demonstrate the point.

The writer is explaining an idea—the nature of what he calls the *comedic vision*. To compare and contrast the *comedic vision* with the *tragic vision* and the *comic vision*, he cites *multiple* examples by way of illustration

    The comic vision has a large gamut, running the range from seeing the amusing incongruities of life to observing the yawning disparities between the ideal and the real and being roused to the harsh satire and black humor of, say, Swift in the fourth part of *Gulliver's Travels*. The comedic vision, however, is entirely different; in fact, it is the obverse of the tragic vision. If the tragic vision sees man as passing from innocence to corruption while forever under the shadow of fatality and death, the comedic vision sees the possibility, even the actuality, of a glorious reversal either here, as in Whitman's "Song of Myself," or hereafter, as in Bunyan's *Pilgrim's Progress*. Not that the comedic vision refuses to recognize the brute facts of man's subjection to fate, his proneness to evil, and the imminence of his death. It simply refuses to settle for this limited view. Instead, it encompasses these facts at the same time that it transcends them. The comedic vision has its own integrity and is an answer to the easy and even posturing despair of modern times.

    The comedic vision has reaches beyond the power of the tragic vision to explore, for, as has been suggested, the tragic vision is self-limiting. It is Dante's *Paradise* rather than his *Inferno*, Shakespeare's *The Tempest* rather than his *Macbeth*, Eliot's *Four Quartets* rather than his *Waste Land*. It is the biblical statement, "The peace of God, which passeth all understanding," as against the despair expressed by Septimius Severus, "I have seen all things and it availed nothing."—From "'Cock-A-Doodle-Doo!' and Some Legends in Melville Scholarship" by Sidney Moss.

The writer is suggesting that there is something very wrong with the world and with his life, an idea he illustrates by *multiple* examples

    My eye ranged over the capacious rolling country, and over the mountains, and over the village, and over a farmhouse here and there, and over woods, groves, streams, rocks, fells—and I thought to myself, what a slight mark, after all, does man make on this huge great earth. Yet the earth makes a mark on him. What a horrid accident was that on the Ohio, where my good friend and thirty other good fellows were sloped into eternity at the bidding of a thick-headed engineer, who knew not a valve from a flue. And that crash on the railroad just over yon mountains there, where two infatuate trains ran pell-mell into each other, and climbed and clawed each other's backs; and one locomotive was found fairly shelled, like a chick, inside of a passenger car in the antagonist train; and near a score of noble hearts, a bride and her groom, and an innocent little infant, were all disembarked into the grim hulk of Charon, who ferried them over, all baggageless, to some clinkered iron-foundry or other. Yet what's the use of complaining? What justice of the peace will right this matter? Yea, what's the use of bothering the very heavens about it? Don't the heavens themselves ordain these things—else they could not happen?

A miserable world! Who would take the trouble to make a fortune in it, when he knows not how long he can keep it, for the thousand villains and asses who have the management of railroads and steamboats, and innumerable other vital things in the world. If they would make me Dictator in North America a while, I'd string them up! and hang, draw, and quarter; fry, roast, and boil; stew, grill, and devil them, like so many turkey-legs—the rascally numskulls of stokers; I'd set them to stokering in Tartarus—I would.

Great improvements of the age! What! to call the facilitation of death and murder an improvement! Who wants to travel so fast? My grandfather did not, and he was no fool. Hark! here comes that old dragon again—that gigantic gad-fly of a Moloch—snort! puff! scream!—here he comes straight-bent through these vernal woods, like the Asiatic cholera cantering on a camel. Stand aside! here he comes, the chartered murderer! the death monopolizer! judge, jury, and hangman all together, whose victims die always without benefit of clergy. For two hundred and fifty miles that iron fiend goes yelling through the land, crying "More! more! more!" Would that fifty conspiring mountains would fall atop of him! And while they were about it, would they would also fall atop of that smaller dunning fiend, my creditor, who frightens the life out of me more than any locomotive—a lantern-jawed rascal, who seems to run on a railroad track, too, and duns me even on Sunday, all the way to church and back, and comes and sits in the same pew with me, and pretending to be polite and hand me the prayer-book opened at the proper place, pokes his pesky bill under my nose in the very midst of my devotions, and so shoves himself between me and salvation; for how can one keep his temper on such occasions?

I can't pay this horrid man; and yet they say money was never so plentiful—a drug in the market; but blame me if I can get any of the drug, though there never was a sick man more in need of that particular sort of medicine. It's a lie; money ain't plentiful—feel of my pocket. Ha! here's a powder I was going to send to the sick baby in yonder hovel, where the Irish ditcher lives. That baby has the scarlet fever. They say the measles are rife in the country, too, and the varioloid, and the chicken-pox, and it's bad for teething children. And after all, I suppose many of the poor little ones, after going through all this trouble, snap off short; and so they had the measles, mumps, croup, scarlet fever, chicken-pox, cholera morbus, summer-complaint, and all else, in vain! Ah! there's that twinge of the rheumatics in my right shoulder. I got it one night on the North River, when, in a crowded boat, I gave up my berth to a sick lady, and stayed on deck till morning in drizzling weather. There's the thanks one gets for charity! Twinge! Shoot away, ye rheumatics! Ye couldn't lay on worse if I were some villain who had murdered the lady instead of befriending her. Dyspepsia too—I am troubled with that.—From "Cock-A-Doodle-Doo!" by Herman Melville.

Single EXAMPLE Statements to Illustrate an Idea

One *example statement* may be sufficient to illustrate an idea. The two selections below demonstrate the point.

Single example statement to illustrate the *idea* of induction (which is the process of reasoning from particular facts to a general conclusion)

Suppose you go into a fruiterer's shop, wanting an apple,—you take up one, and, on biting it, you find it sour; you look at it, and see that it is hard and green. You take up another one, and that too is hard, green, and sour. The shopman offers you a third; but, before biting it, you examine it, and find that it is hard and green, and you immediately say that you will not have it, as it must be sour, like those you have already tried.

Nothing can be more simple than that, you think; but if you will take the trouble to analyze and trace out into its logical elements what has been done by the mind, you will be greatly surprised. In the first place, you have performed the operation of induction. You found that, in two experiences, hardness and greenness in apples went together with sourness. It was so in the first case, and it was confirmed by the second. True, it is a very small basis, but still it is enough to make an induction from; you generalize the facts, and you expect to find sourness in apples where you get hardness and greenness. You found upon that a general law, that all hard and green apples are sour; and that, so far as it goes, is a perfect induction. Well, having got your natural law in this way, when you are offered another apple which you find is hard and green, you say, "All hard and green apples are sour; this apple is hard and green; therefore this apple is sour." That train of reasoning is what logicians called a syllogism, and has all its various parts and terms,—its major premise, its minor premise, and its conclusion.—From *Darwiniana* by Thomas Henry Huxley.

Idea

The whole force of conversation depends on how much you can take for granted.

Single example statement serving as an explanatory *analogy*

Vulgar chess-players have to play their game out; nothing short of the brutality of an actual checkmate satisfies their dull apprehensions. But look at two masters of that noble game! White stands well enough, so far as you can see; but Red says, Mate in six moves;—White looks,—nods;—the game is over.

Application of the *analogy*: first-rate chess players compared with first-rate conversation-alists

Just so in talking with first-rate men, especially when they are good-natured and expansive, as they are apt to be at table.—from *The Autocrat of the Breakfast-Table* by Oliver Wendell Holmes.

Exercises A

1. Would you have gained a clearer idea of *induction* if Huxley had used more than one example, or would multiple examples have confused rather than clarified his explanation? Explain.
2. Should Holmes have used more examples to illustrate what he meant by *good conversationalists*?
3. In the selections above, under *Multiple EXAMPLE Statements to Support an*

Assertion and *Multiple EXAMPLE Statements to Illustrate an Idea*, would the writers have been as convincing or clear if they had used single example statements instead of multiple ones? Explain.

The example statements occurring in the selections you have read enabled their authors, as we said, to support an assertion or illustrate an idea. Their example statements, in the bargain, made otherwise vague statements vivid and dull ones forceful. It is this transformation—from vagueness to vividness and from dullness to forcefulness—that we shall concentrate upon in the example statements that follow.

EXAMPLE Statements to Make Vague Statements Vivid

The first selection labeled "vivid" gains its vividness from an extended analogy; the second selection gains its vividness from a series of images.

vague

Steamboat pilots on the Mississippi had to know the river thoroughly in order to avoid hazards.

vivid

One cannot easily realize what a tremendous thing it is to know every trivial detail of twelve hundred miles of river and know it with absolute exactness. If you will take the longest street in New York, and travel up and down it, conning its features patiently until you know every house and window and lamp-post and big and little sign by heart, and know them so accurately that you can instantly name the one you are abreast of when you are set down at random in that street in the middle of an inky black night, you will then have a tolerable notion of the amount and exactness of a pilot's knowledge who carries the Mississippi River in his head. And then, if you will go on until you know every street-crossing, the character, size, and position of the crossing-stones, and the varying depth of mud in each of these numberless places, you will have some idea of what the pilot must know in order to keep a Mississippi steamer out of trouble. Next, if you will take half of the signs in that long street, and *change their places* once a month, and still manage to know their new positions accurately on dark nights, and keep up with these repeated changes without making any mistakes, you will understand what is required of a pilot's peerless memory by the fickle Mississippi.—From *Life on the Mississippi* by Mark Twain.

vague

An idea occurred to Ichabod Crane when he saw the animals in the barnyard. How delicious they would taste, he thought, when they were cooked.

vivid

[Ichabod Crane's mouth watered when he saw the animals in the barnyard.]. In his devouring mind's eye, he pictured to himself every roasting-pig running about with a pudding in his belly, and an apple in his mouth; the pigeons were snugly put to bed in a comfortable pie, and tucked in with a coverlet of crust; the geese were swimming in their own gravy; and the ducks pairing cosily in dishes, like snug married couples, with a decent competency of onion sauce. In the porkers he saw carved out the future sleek side of bacon and juicy relishing ham; not a turkey but he beheld daintily trussed up, with its gizzard under its wing, and, peradventure, a necklace of savory sausages; and even bright chanticleer himself lay sprawling on his back, in a side-dish, with uplifted claws, as if craving that quarter which his chivalrous spirit disdained to ask while living.—From "The Legend of Sleepy Hollow" by Washington Irving.

EXAMPLE Statements to Make Dull Statements Forceful

The first selection labeled "forceful" gains its forcefulness by illustrating an idea dramatically; the second selection gains its forcefulness from a series of dramatic details.

dull

During a lull in the Battle of the Bulge, I had a bad experience, one that became a symbol of the war for me. It involved a dead girl whose mother, for all I could make out, was going to try to bury her in the frozen ground. The mother made me feel guilty about the girl's death because our artillery had killed her.

forceful

The image I have of the war is like a film I can run or "freeze" at any frame. I took the "film" in the Ardennes. I was looking for a likely place to relieve myself when I saw a woman and a small girl, one pulling, the other pushing, a go-cart weighted with a rough-hewn coffin. Both of them were thinly clad and seemed mindless of the freezing cold as they sought to avoid the craters caused by our recent artillery bombardments. But soon, despite their cautiousness, the cart sank into a small crater that was hidden by snow and would not budge despite their efforts. I went over to help them, but the woman looked at me with hostile eyes. "Keep away," she said in surprisingly good English. "We need no help from you. You Americans!" she went on in sudden bitterness. "All you know is destruction and how to kill. You with your big guns!" The tears came to her eyes. "Why must you send shells where civilians are living? We are supposed to be your allies, not your enemies!" She wept openly now and lifted a wet face to me. "You killed my daughter with your big guns," she cried. The child began to whimper too now. The woman wiped the child's face with her sleeve and began to comfort her. Unable myself to comfort either of them, I stood there another moment, then walked away—from the go-cart stuck in the crater, which I had somehow and guiltily caused, from the girl in the coffin whom I had somehow and guiltily killed, and from the woman and child who would not forget the Americans in all their days.—Adapted from *Thy Men Shall Fall* by Sidney and Samuel Moss.

Most people live such dull lives that I am reminded of the phrases "life-in-death" and "death-in-life."

This event [the execution of John Brown] advertises me that there is such a fact as death,—the possibility of a man's dying. It seems as if no man had ever died in America before; for in order to die you must first have lived. I don't believe in the hearses, and palls, and funerals that they have had. There was no death in the case, because there had been no life; they merely rotted or sloughed off, pretty much as they had rotted or sloughed along. No temple's veil was rent, only a hole dug somewhere. Let the dead bury their dead. The best of them fairly ran down like a clock. . . . I hear a good many pretend that they are going to die, or that they have died, for aught that I know. Nonsense! I'll defy them to do it. They haven't got life enough in them. They'll deliquesce like fungi, and keep a hundred eulogists mopping the spot where they left off. Only half a dozen or so have died since the world began. . . . We make a needless ado about capital punishment,—taking lives, when there is no life to take.—From "A Plea for Captain John Brown" by Henry David Thoreau.

Exercise B

Write a theme in which you use a single extended example statement to illustrate an idea.

12 **Definition** Statements

A theme is an extended definition. Whatever the methodology and whatever the purpose, *why* topics such as "Why High Schools Should Inaugurate a Five-year Program" (pages 16–17) require an extended definition of one's opinion. This can only be done by discussing representative reasons for holding the opinion.

Similarly, a *what* topic such as "Three Major Tenets of John Calvin's Theology" or "The Seven Catholic Sacraments" (pages 26–28) calls for an extended definition—of representative elements in one instance and of all the elements in the other. And what we say about these two basic topics—*why* and *what* topics—has equal application to any combination of them; e.g., *what-what-why* topics.

In a less obvious sense, all themes are in some degree self-definitions in that they define what we believe and what we know.

Apart from the theme as an extended definition or as self-definition, there are statements that sometimes occur in a theme that are definitional in intent, which we shall designate *definition statements*. These definition statements do not serve to provide evidence; their function, instead, is orientative or explanatory.

Examples A:
Definition Statements

1. The American egret is a long-legged wading bird that has a yellow bill and dark legs.
2. *Sounding* is a method used by oceanographers to explore depths they cannot otherwise reach.
3. The study of celestial bodies is called *astronomy*.
4. The word *radar* is the abbreviation for *R*adio *D*etection *a*nd *R*anging.
5. What is a catalyst? When a chemical action proceeds too slowly or too rapidly for our convenience, the process may be hastened or delayed by adding a substance that is found unchanged after the chemical action is over. The substance used for this purpose is called a catalyst. It should be noted that a substance that acts as a catalyst in one reaction may not necessarily act as a catalyst in another reaction.
6. Helium has been called *The Mighty Nothing* because it is tasteless, odorless, colorless, nonflammable, nonexplosive, and nonpoisonous.
7. By *fission* I mean the division of an organism into new organisms as a process of reproduction.

8. By *fission* I mean the splitting of the nucleus of a heavy atom to form the nuclei of lighter atoms.

9. An aristocrat is a member of a hereditary ruling class.

10. Thomas Jefferson used the term *natural aristocrat* to designate a person of virtue and talents.

11. Thomas Jefferson used the term *artificial aristocrat* to designate a person of wealth and hereditary power who is, however, without either virtue or talents; for if he possessed virtue and talents, he would be a *natural aristocrat*.

12. *Self-actualization* is not an equivalent term for *self-fulfillment* or *maturation* or *individualization* because these expressions do not connote what the term self-actualization connotes—namely, that we need consciously, in a self-determining way, to actualize our latent potentialities. As Carl Rogers and Abraham Maslow define the term, self-actualization has more in common with Paul Tillich's "courage to be" and with Emerson's "self-reliance" than with the other terms specified.

13. In reply to Madame Montholon's questions, Napoleon defined his best troops to be "Those that are victorious."

14. When someone said to Talleyrand, the French statesman and diplomat, that the execution of a nobleman was a crime, Talleyrand answered, "It is worse than a crime; it is a blunder."

15. "It's worse than wicked, my dear; it's vulgar."—*Punch*

16. My method is to take the utmost trouble to find the right thing to say, and then to say it with the utmost levity.—George Bernard Shaw.

17. Friends double our joys and halve our griefs.—Adapted from Francis Bacon.

Language is a code. People who have not learned Sanskrit cannot decipher that language, nor can people who have not learned English decipher English. When we say we understand a language, therefore, we are saying that we have decoded it—that, in other words, we are familiar to one degree or another with its diction and syntax. *Diction* has to do with words. When we do not know the *meaning* of words, we usually consult a *dictionary*. Thus, if words are a code, then dictionaries are codebooks. *Syntax* has to do with the arrangement of words so that their combined meaning can be decoded. See *Exercises A* below.

Exercises A

Below are two sets of examples, the first relating to diction, the other to syntax. Judging from the evidence, which of the two speakers has better decoded the English language?

1. *First speaker*: Cheese is the consolidated curd of milk ripened by the process of fermentation.
   Second speaker: Cheese is joyous meat eggs.

2. *First speaker*: It is no use blaming the mirror if you are ugly.
   Second speaker: If you ugly mirror are use the blaming no is it.

For English-speaking people, of course, definitions have much more to do with diction than with syntax. No matter how versed we are in a language, we continually encounter terms we do not understand. This is true for one or more of four reasons: (1) we have not yet decoded the term and must therefore consult a dictionary; (2) the term may have multiple meanings and we may not be familiar with the particular meaning suggested; (3) we understand the term in its dictionary sense but not in the sense encoded by the writer; or (4) the term may be a coinage and does not appear in the dictionary. Below are examples of these four kinds of dictional difficulties.

Examples B:
Four Kinds of Dictional
Difficulties

1. *Terms used in a dictionary or public sense*
   a. Illative (expressing or introducing an inference: descriptive of such words as *therefore*, *hence*, and *so*).
   b. Sagittate (in the shape of an arrowhead: descriptive of the shape of certain leaves, for instance).
   c. Sciolism (shallow or false knowledge).
2. *Term having multiple meanings*
   a. The horse ran *fast*.
   b. *Fast* colors are those that do not run.
   c. Stand *fast*.
   d. You really ought to *fast* today.
   e. She has the reputation of being a *fast* woman.
   f. He is *fast* with a dollar.
   g. It was a *fast* track.
   h. She is *fast* asleep.
   i. My watch is *fast*.
   j. They were *fast* friends.
   k. He uses *fast* film.
   l. It held *fast*.
   m. In summer we are on *fast* time.
   n. He's living a *fast* life.
   o. He lives *fast* by the river.

   A word belonging to this set should not be regarded as one word but as many words that happen to be spelled alike.
3. *Terms used in a privately encoded sense*
   a. *Ouch* shall represent the class of painful responses.
   b. All of nature is divided into the *Me* and the *non-Me* (adapted from Emerson).
   c. *The Apocalyptic* is one who foresees catastrophe and believes it cannot be avoided; *the Prophet* is one who foresees catastrophe but believes it can be avoided (adapted from Martin Buber).
4. *Coined terms not yet in the dictionary*
   a. Grok
   b. Jabberwocky
   c. Hobbit

When a term is familiar and used in the ordinary dictionary sense, or if the term is sufficiently clear in context, we may assume that the term requires no definition on our part. If we did not make this assumption, we would be reduced to the absurd position of having to define the very first word we use, and then the words we use to define the first word, and so on, losing more ground the more we try to advance. There are only three occasions, then, when we have to provide definitions for our readers: (1) when we believe a key term is unfamiliar to them (*DNA* may be an instance); or (2) when we have adapted a familiar term for a private purpose (*patron*, for instance); or (3) when we encode a term to take on public meaning (such as *the fallacy of thematic interpretation*). These three kinds of terms are exemplified below. Notice that a definition may range from a single sentence to an entire essay (to an entire book, for that matter, such as *The Organization Man* by William H. Whyte, Jr.).

Examples C:
Three Kinds of Terms
Requiring Definition

1. An unfamiliar term

DNA (deoxyribonucleic acid) is the genetic program that determines not only the particular characteristics of an individual; it determines too whether that individual is to be, among the fantastic possibilities of life, a plant, insect, fish, bird, or mammal, for instance.

2. A familiar term defined in a private sense

Is not a patron[*] . . . one who looks with unconcern on a man struggling for life in the water and, when he has reached ground, encumbers him with help?—From Samuel Johnson's letter to Lord Chesterfield.

3. A term encoded to take on public meaning

To make my term *the fallacy of thematic interpretation* intelligible, I shall first cite the evidence, both internal and external, for the argument that Poe's *Narrative of Arthur Gordon Pym* consists of two separate tales that were speciously yoked together to form a "novel."

[The citation of evidence is eliminated here.]

If all this is true and *Pym* consists of two different stories, what shall we do with the unsettling fact that critics have found a theme common to both parts? Literature, needless to say, is not arithmetic that admits of single correct answers. At the same time, however, some rigor in interpretation is required if literary texts are not to serve as inkblot tests. The fact that a common thematic denominator can be found for a multitude of disparate episodes indicates, to be sure, a certain ingenuity on the part of the finder; it does not necessarily indicate that the work itself is, as one such finder put it, "strictly organized and skillfully developed." To determine points of organization and development, one has to examine the many elements of the story. It is too easy, not to say misleading, to rest one's critical case on theme alone. Any critic who deals with a variety of novels knows that he can find a theme common to most, if not all, of them. His findings are limited only by his cleverness. To take a case, *Crime and Punishment* and *The Scarlet Letter* are totally different in narrative intention, in narrative technique, in characterization, and in structure, though both novels uniquely treat a common theme—the effect of sin upon sinners. Yet, literary collections, to belabor the point somewhat, are continually appearing under such common theme labels as "The Battle of the Sexes" and "Plays of Crime and Punishment."

None of this is to deny that literary works, and Poe's in particular, make a

*A patron, in the ordinary dictionary sense, is usually a wealthy and influential person (as Lord Chesterfield was) who sponsors and supports a poor and unrecognized artist (such as Johnson was at the outset).

powerful appeal to the subliminal senses. Perhaps it is finally on this score that as critics we feel urged to explain how the appeal was achieved and the special nature of our response to it. But to engage in thematic interpretation while brushing aside all other narrative elements as inconsequential seems a fallacious procedure indeed. To "make a case," to concern oneself exclusively with theme, is to make the reality of the work what the critic ordains it to be. We may learn a great deal about the critic's psyche in this way, but what we learn about the literary work is another question.

Poe as writer and critic was, of course, aware of this fallacy of interpretation and derided it accordingly. "Every fiction," he wrote, "*should have* a moral"—*moral* was his word for *theme*—"and, what is more to the purpose, the critics have discovered that every fiction has. . . . These fellows demonstrate a hidden meaning in 'The Antediluvians' [a book-length poem by James McHenry which, in its time, was called a "tuneless abortion"], . . . new views in 'Cock Robin' and transcendentalism in 'Hop O' My Thumb.' In short, it has been shown that no man can sit down to write without a very profound design. Thus to authors in general much trouble is spared. A novelist, for example, need have no care of his moral. It is there—that is to say it is somewhere—and the moral and the critic can take care of themselves. When the proper time arrives, all that the gentleman intended, and all that he did not intend, will be brought to light, in the 'Dial,' or the 'Down-Easter,' together with all that he ought to have intended, and the rest that he clearly meant to intend;—so that it will all come very straight in the end. There is no just ground, therefore, for the charge brought against me by certain ignoramuses—that I have never written a moral tale, or, in more precise words, a tale with a moral. They are not the critics predestined to bring me out, and *develop* my morals;—that is the secret. By and by the 'North American Quarterly Humdrum' will make them ashamed of their stupidity."—From "*Arthur Gordon Pym*, or The Fallacy of Thematic Interpretation" by Sidney Moss.

Exercises B

1. Some terms such as *golf*, *reflex action*, *covered bridge*, and *golden bantam corn* have largely public meanings. Other terms such as *beautiful*, *excessive*, *obscene*, *delinquent*, and *radical* have largely private meanings. For instance, you may consider a person *fanatic*; another may regard him as *dedicated*. Which of the terms below have largely public meaning? Which largely private meaning?
   a. Law of gravity
   b. Funny
   c. Incubation
   d. Intolerable
   e. Dialectical materialism
   f. Obsessional neurosis
   g. Maturity
   h. Pleasurable
   i. Multiple linear regression
   j. Desirable
2. *Greech* is a non-word in the sense that it has at this moment neither a public nor private meaning, for we have just coined the word for this exercise.

We shall now put *greech* into a number of contexts, which will serve to encode it (to make a word of this non-word). Read the statements below and decode (define) *greech*.

a.   His sense of greech is perfect; he has no enemies and many friends.

b.   Greech is the only means of solving the problems of human relations.

c.   "Practice greech, my son," saith the sage; "it pleaseth him that doth give and him that doth receive it."

d.   Greech should be exercised on all occasions, not only at Christmas time.

3. Write a 300- to 400-word theme in which you *define* one of the following public terms or, at the discretion of your instructor, a public term of your own choice. Notice that these terms represent *what* topics for which *example statements* may have to be adduced.

a.   Consciousness-raising

b.   Phenomenology

c.   Self-actualization

d.   Semantics

e.   Fortran (or any other computer-science language)

f.   The Salk vaccine (or any other recent discovery in science)

g.   Behavior modification

h.   The oil cartel

i.   The Equal Rights Amendment

j.   Dialectical materialism

k.   Cubism (or any other movement in art)

l.   Absurdism (or any other philosophical outlook)

m.   The quartet (or any other form of musical composition)

n.   Situation ethics

o.   The open classroom

p.   Transactional analysis

q.   Plato's Allegory of the Cave

r.   The new conservatism

s.   The federal court system

13 Review of the Nature of Evidence

To provide the class with an opportunity to engage in a full-scale review of the nature of evidence, a selection for analysis, drawn from Charles Dickens' *American Notes*, appears below. In reading the selection, identify all the kinds of evidence that Dickens introduces and determine how persuasive he is.

Background Information

Nearly thirty years of age and already the most popular author of his time, Charles Dickens decided to visit the United States. In preparing for his tour, he read a great number of travel books written by his compatriots who had been to the United States, but he resisted their influence, they were so critical of America and so chilling of his expectations.

From the time of his arrival in the States in January 1842, Dickens was celebrated as perhaps no person in America, native or foreign, had ever been celebrated before, including George Washington and General Lafayette. William Cullen Bryant in his *New York Evening Post* felt that the ovations to Dickens "may have been carried too far"; nevertheless, he rejoiced that "a young man, without birth, wealth, title, or a sword, whose only claims to distinction are in his intellect and heart, is received with a feeling that was formerly rendered only to emperors and kings. . . . The author, by his genius, has contributed happy moments to the lives of thousands, and it is only right that the thousands should recompense the gift."

Despite this celebration, Dickens, only one month in America, wrote to an English friend that if a man were not a "radical on principle, . . . he would return home [from America] a tory," because republicanism, *as practiced* in America, was bound to deal "the heaviest blow ever dealt at liberty . . . in the failure of its example to the earth." To another English friend he wrote with similar disappointment: "This is not the Republic I came to see. . . . I infinitely prefer a liberal Monarchy . . . to such a [republican] Government as this. . . . And England, even England, bad and faulty as the old land is, and miserable as millions of her people are, rises in comparison."

When Dickens returned to London in June 1842, he began to record his impressions of the United States for a book called *American Notes*, which was published in October of that year. The book became in the States perhaps the most unpopular best seller ever written, for in his "Concluding Remarks," not to speak of his chapter on "Slavery," he was, with some qualification, very critical of America, especially of what he called the "Universal Distrust" of the

people, their "love of 'smart' dealing," and their "love of trade." What offended him most, however, was the American newspaper press, which he
called a "monster of depravity." He wished that the American people would
come to love "the Real less, and the Ideal somewhat more," a love that would
be expressed in "greater . . . lightness of heart and gayety, and a wider cultivation of what is beautiful, without being eminently and directly useful."

The excerpt below is from "Concluding Remarks," the final chapter of *American Notes*. In reading this excerpt, identify all the kinds of evidence that
Dickens introduces and determine how persuasive he is.

Charles Dickens' "Concluding Remarks" from *American Notes*

I may be pardoned, if on such a theme as the general character of the American
people, and the general character of their social system, as presented to a
stranger's eyes, I desire to express my own opinions. . . .

They are, by nature, frank, brave, cordial, hospitable, and affectionate. Cultivation and refinement seem but to enhance their warmth of heart and ardent
enthusiasm; and it is the possession of these latter qualities in a most remarkable degree, which renders an educated American one of the most endearing
and most generous of friends. I never was so won upon, as by this class; never
yielded up my full confidence and esteem so readily and pleasurably, as to
them; never can make again, in half a year, so many friends for whom I seem
to entertain the regard of half a life.

These qualities are natural, I implicitly believe, to the whole people. That
they are, however, sadly sapped and blighted in their growth among the mass;
and that there are influences at work which endanger them still more, and
give but little present promise of their healthy restoration; is a truth that ought
to be told.

It is an essential part of every national character to pique itself mightily upon
its faults, and to deduce tokens of its virtue or its wisdom from their very exaggeration. One great blemish in the popular mind of America, and the prolific
parent of an innumerable brood of evils, is Universal Distrust. Yet, the American citizen plumes himself upon this spirit, even when he is sufficiently dis-
passionate to perceive the ruin it works; and will often adduce it, in spite of
his own reason, as an instance of the great sagacity and acuteness of the people, and their superior shrewdness and independence.

"You carry," says the stranger, "this jealousy and distrust into every trans-
action of public life. By repelling worthy men from your legislative assemblies,
it has bred up a class of candidates for the suffrage, who, in their every act,
disgrace your Institutions and your people's choice. It has rendered you so
fickle, and so given to change, that your inconstancy has passed into a prov-
erb, for you no sooner set up an idol firmly, than you are sure to pull it down
and dash it into fragments; and this, because directly you reward a benefactor,
or a public servant, you distrust him, merely because he *is* rewarded; and
immediately apply yourselves to find out, either that you have been too boun-
tiful in your acknowledgements, or he remiss in his deserts. Any man who
attains a high place among you, from the President downward, may date his
downfall from that moment; for any printed lie that any notorious villain pens,
although it militate directly against the character and conduct of a life, appeals
at once to your distrust, and is believed. You will strain at a gnat in the way of
trustfulness and confidence, however fairly won and well deserved; but you

will swallow a whole caravan of camels, if they be laden with unworthy doubts and mean suspicions. Is this well, think you, or likely to elevate the character of the governors or the governed among you?"

The answer is invariably the same: "There's freedom of opinion here, you know. Every man thinks for himself, and we are not to be easily overreached. That's how our people come to be suspicious."

Another prominent feature is the love of "smart" dealing, which gilds over many a swindle and gross breach of trust; many a defalcation, public and private; and enables many a knave to hold his head up with the best, who well deserves a halter—though it has not been without its retributive operation, for this smartness has done more in a few years to impair the public credit, and to cripple the public resources, than dull honesty, however rash, could have effected in a century. The merits of a broken speculation, or a bankruptcy, or of a successful scoundrel, are not gauged by its or his observance of the golden rule, "Do as you would be done by," but are considered with reference to their smartness. I recollect, on both occasions of our passing that ill-fated Cairo on the Mississippi remarking on the bad effects such gross deceits must have when they exploded, in generating a want of confidence abroad, and discouraging foreign investment; but I was given to understand that this was a very smart scheme by which a deal of money had been made; and that its smartest feature was, that they forgot these things abroad in a very short time, and speculated again as freely as ever. The following dialogue I have held a hundred times: "Is it not a very disgraceful circumstance that such a man as So-and-so should be acquiring a large property by the most infamous and odious means, and, notwithstanding all the crimes of which he has been guilty, should be tolerated and abetted by your citizens? He is a public nuisance, is he not?" "Yes, sir." "A convicted liar?" "Yes, sir." "He has been kicked, and cuffed, and caned?" "Yes, sir." "And he is utterly dishonourable, debased, and profligate?" "Yes, sir." "In the name of wonder, then, what is his merit?" "Well, sir, he is a smart man."

In like manner, all kinds of deficient and impolitic usages are referred to the national love of trade; though, oddly enough, it would be a weighty charge against a foreigner, that he regarded the Americans as a trading people. The love of trade is assigned as a reason for that comfortless custom, so very prevalent in country towns, of married persons living in hotels, having no fireside of their own, and seldom meeting from early morning until late at night, but at the hasty public meals. The love of trade is a reason why the literature of America is to remain forever unprotected: "For we are a trading people, and don't care for poetry," though we *do*, by-the-way, profess to be very proud of our poets; while healthful amusements, cheerful means of recreation, and wholesome fancies, must fade before the stern utilitarian joys of trade.

These three characteristics are strongly presented at every turn, full in the stranger's view. But the foul growth of America has a more tangled root than this, and it strikes its fibres deep in its licentious Press.

Schools may be erected East, West, North, and South; pupils be taught, and masters reared, by scores upon scores of thousands; colleges may thrive, churches may be crammed, temperance may be diffused, and advancing knowledge in all other forms walk through the land with giant strides; but, while the newspaper press of America is in, or near, its present abject state, high moral improvement in that country is hopeless. Year by year it must and will go back; year by year the tone of public feeling must sink lower down; year by year the Congress and the Senate must become of less account before all decent men; and, year by year, the memory of the Great Fathers of the Revolution must be outraged more and more in the bad life of their degenerate child.

Among the herd of journals which are published in the States, there are some, the reader scarcely need be told, of character and credit. From personal intercourse with accomplished gentlemen connected with publications of this class I have derived both pleasure and profit. But the name of these is Few, and of the others Legion; and the influence of the good is powerless to counteract the mortal poison of the bad.

Among the gentry of America; among the well-informed and moderate; in the learned professions; at the bar and on the bench, there is, as there can be, but one opinion in reference to the vicious character of these infamous journals. It is sometimes contended—I will not say strangely, for it is natural to seek excuses for such a disgrace—that their influence is not so great as a visiter would suppose. I must be pardoned for saying that there is no warrant for this plea, and that every fact and circumstance tends directly to the opposite conclusion.

When any man, of any grade of desert in intellect or character, can climb to any public distinction, no matter what, in America, without first grovelling down upon the earth, and bending the knee before this monster of depravity; when any private excellence is safe from its attacks, and when any social confidence is left unbroken by it, or any tie of social decency and honour is held in the least regard; when any man in that Free Country has freedom of opinion, and presumes to think for himself, and speak for himself, without humble reference to a censorship which, for its rampant ignorance and base dishonesty, he utterly loathes and despises in his heart; when those who most acutely feel its infamy and the reproach it casts upon the nation, and who most denounce it to each other, dare to set their heels upon and crush it openly, in the sight of all men; then, I will believe that its influence is lessening, and men are returning to their manly senses. But while that Press has its evil eye in every house, and its black hand in every appointment in the state, from a president to a postman; while, with ribald slander for its only stock in trade, it is the standard literature of an enormous class, who must find their reading in a newspaper, or they will not read at all; so long must its odium be upon the country's head, and so long must the evil it works, be plainly visible in the Republic.

To those who are accustomed to the leading English Journals, or to the respectable journals of the Continent of Europe; to those who are accustomed to anything else in print and paper; it would be impossible, without an amount of extract for which I have neither space nor inclination, to convey an adequate idea of this frightful engine in America. But if any man desire confirmation of my statement on this head, let him repair to any place in this city of London where scattered numbers of these publications are to be found; and there let him form his own opinion.

It would be well, there can be no doubt, for the American people as a whole, if they loved the Real less, and the Ideal somewhat more. It would be well, if there were greater encouragement to lightness of heart and gayety, and a wider cultivation of what is beautiful, without being eminently and directly useful. But then, I think the general remonstrance, "we are a new country," which is so often advanced as an excuse for defects which are quite unjustifiable, as being, of right, only the slow growth of an old one, may be very reasonably urged; and I yet hope to hear of there being some other national amusement in the United States, besides newspaper politics.

They certainly are not a humorous people, and their temperament always impressed me as being of a dull and gloomy character. In shrewdness of remark, and a certain cast-iron quaintness, the Yankees, or people of New-England, unquestionably take the lead; as they do in most other evidences of intelligence. But in travelling about, out of the large cities, as I have remarked in former parts of this volume; I was quite oppressed by the prevailing seriousness and melancholy air of business: which was so general and unvarying, that at every new town I came to, I seemed to meet the very same people whom I had left behind me, at the last. Such defects as are perceptibly in the national manners, seem, to me, to be referable, in a great degree, to this cause: which has generated a dull, sullen persistence in coarse usages, and rejected the graces of life as undeserving of attention. There is no doubt that Washington, who was always most scrupulous and exact on points of ceremony, perceived the tendency towards this mistake, even in his time; and did his utmost to correct it. . . .

The Republican Institutions of America undoubtedly lead the people to assert their self-respect and their equality; but a traveller is bound to bear those Institutions in his mind, and not hastily to resent the near approach of a class of strangers, who, at home, would keep aloof. This characteristic, when it was tinctured with no foolish pride, and stopped short of no honest service, never offended me: and I very seldom, if ever, experienced its rude or unbecoming display. Once or twice it was comically developed, as in the following case: but this was an amusing incident, and not the rule nor near it.

I wanted a pair of boots at a certain town, for I had none to travel in, but those with the memorable cork soles, which were much too hot for the fiery decks of a steamboat. I therefore sent a message to an artist in boots, importing, with my compliments, that I should be happy to see him, if he would do me the polite favour to call. He very kindly returned for answer that he would "look round" at six o'clock that evening.

I was lying on the sofa, with a book and a wineglass, at about that time, when the door opened, and a gentleman in a stiff cravat, within a year or two on either side of thirty, entered, in his hat and gloves; walked up to the looking-glass; arranged his hair; took off his gloves; slowly produced a measure from the uttermost depths of his coat-pocket; and requested me, in a languid tone, to "unfix" my straps. I complied, but looked with some curiosity at his hat, which was still upon his head. It might have been that, or it might have been the heat—but he took it off. Then he sat himself down on a chair opposite to me; rested an arm on each knee; and, leaning forward very much, took from the ground, by a great effort, the specimen of metropolitan workmanship which I had just pulled off—whistling, pleasantly, as he did so. He turned it over and over; surveyed it with a contempt no language can express; and inquired if I wished him to fix me a boot like *that*? I courteously replied, that provided the boots were large enough, I would leave the rest to him; that if convenient and practicable, I should not object to their bearing some resemblance to the model then before him; but that I would be entirely guided by, and would beg to leave the whole subject to his judgment and discretion. "You an't partickler about this scoop in the heel, I suppose then?" says he: "we don't foller that, here." I repeated my last observation. He looked at himself in the glass again; went closer to it to dash a grain or two of dust out of the corner of his eye; and settled his cravat. All this time, my leg and foot were in the air. "Nearly ready, sir?" I inquired. "Well, pretty nigh," he said; "keep steady." I kept as steady as I could, both in foot and face; and having by this time got the dust out, and found his pencil-case, he measured me, and made the necessary notes. When he had finished, he fell into his old attitude, and taking up the boot again, mused for some time. "And this," he said, at last, "is an English boot, is it? This is a London boot, eh?" "That, sir," I replied, "is a London boot." He mused over it again, after the manner of Hamlet with Yorick's scull; nodded his head, as who should say "I pity the institutions that led to the production of this boot!" rose; put up his pencil, notes, and paper —glancing at himself in the glass, all the time—put on his hat, drew on his gloves very slowly, and finally walked out. When he had been gone about a minute, the door reopened, and his hat and his head reappeared. He looked round the room, and at the boot again, which was still lying on the floor; appeared thoughtful for a minute; and then said, "Well, good arternoon." "Good afternoon, sir," said I; and that was the end of the interview. . . .

I have now arrived at the close of this book. I have little reason to believe, from certain warnings I have had since I returned to England, that it will be tenderly or favourably received by the American people; and as I have written the truth in relation to the mass of those who form their judgment and express their opinions, it will be seen that I have no desire to court, by any adventitious means, the popular applause.

It is enough for me to know, that what I have set down in these pages, cannot cost me a single friend on the other side of the Atlantic, who is, in anything, deserving of the name. For the rest, I put my trust implicitly in the spirit in which they have been conceived and penned, and I can bide my time.

I have made no reference to my reception, nor have I suffered it to influence me in what I have written; for, in either case, I should have offered but a sorry acknowledgment, compared with that I bear within my breast, towards those partial readers of my former books across the water, who met me with an open hand, and not with one that closed upon an iron muzzle.

Index